The Battle of Woody Point: The History of the Confrontat[...] Deaths of the First American Settlers in the Pacific Northwest

By Charles River Editors

ATTACK AND MASSACRE OF CREW OF SHIP TONQUIN BY THE SAVAGES OF THE N.W.COAST

A depiction of the natives boarding the *Tonquin* before the attack

About Charles River Editors

Charles River Editors is a boutique digital publishing company, specializing in bringing history back to life with educational and engaging books on a wide range of topics. Keep up to date with our new and free offerings with this 5 second sign up on our weekly mailing list, and visit Our Kindle Author Page to see other recently published Kindle titles.

We make these books for you and always want to know our readers' opinions, so we encourage you to leave reviews and look forward to publishing new and exciting titles each week.

Introduction

ASTORIA, AS IT WAS IN 1813.

A contemporary depiction of Fort Astoria

In 1801, Thomas Jefferson took office as the third President of the United States. His first term began scarcely a quarter century after completing the transformation of a new alliance of states to an official national government and a recognized international entity. However, the nation's inner ratification of its own identity provided little protection from a host of European powers bent on augmenting their empires in an age of expansionism. Geographically, the U.S. maintained only a foothold on the massive North American continent, in the center of what one historian described as a "scramble"[1] for international trade and territory. Jefferson shared this ideal as the norm of his era, a "western imperial vision"[2] that all but required the acquisition of territory for both economic prosperity and security. Britain's defeat at Yorktown was not by any means the end of the trans-Atlantic conflict, and the vast remainder of the North American continent was claimed by "a bewildering array"[3] of overseas powers, the most prominent of which was Britain. Uncertain southern borders to American states and territories were manned by Spanish forces as well, while Scottish interests explored the vast western portion of present-day Canada. Even the Irish maneuvered for land claims in an exploration frenzy that extended from England to Russia.

---

[1] *James P. Ronda, Astoria and Empire, Review by Reginald C. Stuart, The International History Review, Vol. 14, No. 1 (February 1991) p. 136*

[2] *James P. Ronda*

[3] *James P. Ronda, Astoria and the Birth of Empire, Montana: The Magazine of Western History, Vol. 36 No. 3 (Summer 1986), pp. 22-25*

By Jefferson's third year of office, the U.S. felt the discomfort of impending war with France, which had so recently assisted the Americans in their separation from the British Empire. For Jefferson, the remedy was to be found in the purchase of New Orleans, an obvious point of attack if the French chose to invade the North American continent. Envoys were sent to Paris to effect the purchase of the city, but inexplicably returned with the entire center section of the western continent instead, directly east of the states under American ownership. The massive real estate deal, to some extent a shock to the American system by its scope suddenness, was accomplished for a mere cost of $15,000,000 dollars.

The 800,000 square miles of land were originally ceded to France by Spain. Napoleon had his own share of problems with entanglements closer to home, and would soon have his hands full with the British Royal Navy. He therefore released ownership of the Louisiana Territory with surprisingly little coaxing. The acquisition doubled the geographic area of the United States. This stood in direct philosophical conflict with a president who above all else loathed the thought of federal power presiding over domestic matters. However, as part of Jefferson's ethical dilemma, the thought of an American state spanning the entire continent was alluring.

Such a state was not only the dream of Jefferson. From the early 19th century, the image of an American empire extending to both coasts became a rallying cry. The Pacific Ocean represented, in Jefferson's mind, the most effective western border. His view was in part inaccurate, as he expected the Rocky Mountains to resemble the gentler Appalachians, not a range of American Alps.

Governing from the Eastern seaboard, the two most effective methods of procuring wilderness lands in the west necessitated a campaign of exploration and the establishment of permanent trade entities located in strategic locations to discourage invasion and enhance internationalism. The first was accomplished by a two-year expedition from St. Louis to the Pacific Ocean under the leadership of Captain Meriwether Lewis and William Clark. From 1804 to 1806, the expedition gathered information on land and river routes to the western coast, with an eye toward trade and settlement. The party wintered at the mouth of the Columbia River, at what is now known as Fort Clatsop. The Corps of Discovery's report to Jefferson enumerated the difficulties in reaching the Pacific, but spoke glowingly of the land as a resource. Although the waterway to the west was not an unbroken route as hoped, Lewis and Clark suggested that furs and other non-fragile items could be transported across the continent at minimal cost, crossing the Rocky Mountains by pack horse, and continuing east on the Missouri River system. Through interaction with various indigenous tribes and by direct evidence, they further claimed that the western continent was an unowned country "richer in beaver than any other country on earth.[4]"

---

[4] *History.com, 1810, The Pacific Fur Company's First Ship Leaves for Oregon – www.history.com/this-day-in-history/the-pacific-fur-cmpanys-first-ship-leaves-for-oregon*

The idea of interior trade to the East Coast soon expanded to regular transactions with Asian countries, primarily China. Such a plan meant an exchange of foreign products as well, with exotic items finding their way back to New York markets. Dealing with China represented both a lower cost and a lower likelihood of conflict than the U.S. risked in trade with Britain and France. Jefferson's imagination was, to that point, preoccupied with the seagoing aspect of global relations. Two years prior to the Lewis and Clark expedition, he read James Cook's *A Voyage to the Pacific Ocean* and was tantalized by Alexander MacKenzie's *Voyages from Montreal*. MacKenzie had completed a successful voyage throughout much of the Pacific Ocean in the last decade of the 18th century and survived two epic voyages to the Arctic region four years later. One historical account characterizes MacKenzie as a man "filled with passion for making discoveries,"[5] adding that he had attempted for years to coax Britain into ventures along the western American coast. Jefferson was, in particular, struck by MacKenzie's zeal for potential commerce along the Columbia River, an enormous stream discovered near the end of the 18th century by Boston sailing master Robert Gray. Many historians believe that, through increased knowledge of western voyages and potential trade establishments, Jefferson was "jolted"[6] into a sense of geography more attuned to the perspective of hemispheres than to small land regions. Along with MacKenzie's accounts, it was Meriwether Lewis who most earnestly proposed a trading fort on the Columbia. Jefferson, however, clung to his distaste for federal financing until it became ultimately impractical to resist such an investment.

The second push, to establish trade with the numerous western tribes and to found a fort only a few miles from Clatsop, followed soon after as a precursor to the indigenous American and Asian connection. The U.S. was fortunate to possess a premier talent in John Jacob Astor, a man already experienced in trade with overseas clients. Astor, a German-born immigrant from the town of Waldorf, showed little spark for business as the third son of a butcher, but as a fur trader, real estate investor, and leading businessman of his era, he soon rose to become the dominant figure in Jefferson's strategic trade plan and easily the wealthiest American of the early 19th century.

Astor's ambitions came at a time when the Hudson's Bay Company operated like a virtual empire within an empire, and it held an almost absolute monopoly on trade across most of British North America. From the 1780s onwards, however, it faced vigorous competition from a new rival in the form of the North West Company, based out of Montreal. Blocked out of the most lucrative fur regions of British North America, the North West Company had established itself in the Pacific Northwest and pushed aggressively westward, creating the first European settlements and outposts among the native tribes of the Columbia territory. In part, President Jefferson's objective in sponsoring the Lewis and Clark Expedition was to find a way to direct this growing trade into the United States, rather than north into British territory or west across

---

[5] *James P. Ronda*

[6] *James P. Ronda*

the ocean. As Lewis and Clark returned to St. Louis, the North West Company was already exploring New Caledonia, comprising most of modern-day British Columbia. None of this was formal British territory, but along with most of the coast above the 42nd Parallel, it formed part of Britain's claim, and the companies active therein tended to reinforce this fact.

In 1808, North West Company explorer Alexander Mackenzie traced the great Canadian river now bearing his name to the Arctic Ocean, disappointed that it did not empty, as expected, into the Pacific Ocean. This, however, was further incentive to look south and west, and at about the same time, North West Company trader and explorer David Thompson undertook a series of journeys of exploration that opened up a vast new territory comprising the upper Columbia River, British Columbia, Idaho and Montana.

From the other direction came Astor, who watched the competition with a keen eye and learned a great deal from the establishment of the North West Company. The personnel of the various fur companies in the New World often kept close company. In the unpopulated wild, they depended on one another as protection against isolation and even collaborated in some circumstances. However, Astor wanted a monopoly on the Pacific Northwest, where all trade with the Indians could be carried out through one company. To accomplish that, he had to accelerate Jefferson's thinking and begin the process quickly before the North West Company caught wind of it and intruded.

Thus, in 1810, through the Pacific Fur Company, Astor began to direct his energies at the still mostly unexploited regions accessible from the mouth of the Columbia River. This was, of course, in open defiance of British claims, but that was very much in keeping with Astor's style. Astor put up the money, and a group of American and Canadian fur traders would manage affairs on the ground, traveling to the region to erect Fort Astoria and a string of trading posts in the region that could deal with the natives, trade with Asia and the East Coast, and amass untold riches. Or at least that was the plan.

Fort Astoria wouldn't last a decade, and its turbulent history was so full of unfortunate twists and turns, a mixture of bad luck and incompetence, that the story still fascinates people today. And among all the chapters of that short history, none are as interesting as the fateful Battle of Woody Point, a misnomer for a confrontation that was brought about by misunderstandings, arrogance, and misplaced pride. The episode, despite its brevity and its occurrence in the furthest reaches of North America at the time, would color relations between whites and natives in the Pacific Northwest for decades.

The Battle of Woody Point: The History of the Confrontation that Led to the Deaths of the First American Settlers in the Pacific Northwest

The Fur Industry

Beavers were of vital importance to the hat trade for centuries. There are two species of beaver: the Eurasian beaver (*Castor fibes*) and the North American beaver (*Castor canadensis*). European beavers were scarce in the era with which this book is concerned, and they were driven to extinction in much of Europe by the early hat trade, but populations survived in northern Scandinavia and Russia.

What makes the beaver of such importance to the fur trade is not the beaver pelts themselves, but their undercoat. A beaver's coat consists of long guard hairs and an undercoat of shorter hair, particularly dense in winter and denser in beavers during winter in northern climates. The outer guard hair has to be removed, and the dense undercoat is shaved off. Sometimes called "beaver wool," this material makes the finest felt, which is then processed into hats. A beaver hat keeps its shape, its warm and sturdy, it repels water, and it can last for many years. Wearing a beaver hat marked social class because they were expensive. Beaver hat styles included floppy hats with plumes worn by Cavaliers, Abraham Lincoln's stovepipe top hat, and today's Stetson cowboy hat.

Beavers can seem like cartoonish animals with their strange flat tails and huge buck teeth, but in their way, beavers were a keystone species in North America. Before the European intrusions, beavers populated areas from the Rio Grande to the Arctic and over most of the continent, save deserts and marshy areas like Florida. Estimates of the total beaver population range from 40,000,000 to 400,000,000. The key thing about beavers is that they build dams. Millions of beavers meant millions of beaver dams, which quite literally dammed streams. The dams created ponds in which the beavers make sturdy, thick dens that are entered from underwater. They store plenty of sticks and limbs underwater and spend the winter under the ice in the den. These characteristics give beavers a great deal of protection from predators, but not from humans. Beaver dams can be quite large, as can the ponds created by the dams. The longest beaver dam known in recent decades was about 2,800 feet, or a half-mile (Backhouse 14).

The creation of beaver ponds has quite a large ecological impact. Trees trapped in the ponds die, creating habitats for many kinds of birds. The ponds release water slowly, evening out water flow, and many beaver ponds in an area help to regulate groundwater flow to the aquifer. Ponds create habitats for weeds and other vegetation preferred by species such as deer. Abandoned ponds gradually fill in, becoming marshy and then meadows, habitats conducive to grazing species and farming (Backhouse 6).

A characteristic of beavers is the scent glands they use to mark their territory that secrete a substance called castoreum. Hunters (and later trappers, when metal traps became available) baited sticks with castoreum. Beavers are quite territorial, and they have an excellent sense of smell, so they would come quickly to investigate the new smell. The substance was also used for medicine, as it was thought to cure or help cure colic, toothaches, deafness, sciatica, liver tumors, trembling, poisoning, and pleurisy. It may actually have helped some of these conditions because it contains salicylic acid, the main ingredient in aspirin (Dolin 325).

The European beaver species had a considerable ecological impact as well, but it has not been as widely studied as the North American species. They were nearly wiped out in most of Europe because of the demand for furs, and by the 1600s, they were relegated to Europe and Russia's far north. Consequently, there were fewer observations about the North American beavers and their impact, though the species was richly chronicled by traders, travelers, and groups such as the French Jesuits.

Beaver hats were handmade and still are. Making them requires skill, and the process is complicated, but the basic fact is that a beaver's undercoat makes a superb felt for hat-making. Beavers have two kinds of hair. The coarse, outer coat is long and called guard hair, and the other hair is short and dense. The difficulty lies in getting rid of the long guard hairs. Beaver hair, like all hair, has a keratin coat. After processing, the hairs mat together to make a superior felt that is better and stronger than felt made from other furs.

The outer guard hair coat has to be combed out, which is a laborious process. It is also what made "coat beaver" so valuable. Native Americans wore beaver coats with the fur inside, which exposed it to human sweat and body oils, softening the fur and making the guard hair easy to remove. Once the undesirable long hair was removed, the dense underfur was shaved from the skin, resulting in a ball of fur called beaver wool or beaver fluff. The fluff then went through a process called "carroting" in which a solution of mercury salts dissolved in nitric acid was applied to the fluff, dissolving some of the keratin on the hair, making it easier to felt and turning the beaver wool to a shade of orange, hence the term "carroting" (Feinstein).

Following carroting, the fluff was laid on a table pierced with holes. A skilled worker then used a tool called a Hatter's bow, looking like a distorted violin bow, which he moved over the fluff while vibrating the string, causing the fluff to mat further together and dirt to drop through the holes in the table. At the end of this process, the loosely felted material is called a "batt." It took two large batts to make the core of a hat, and two smaller ones for the brim and other features. The two batts were placed on top of one another under a wet cloth or wet leather, and heat was applied, resulting in further felting and some shrinkage (Feinstein).

Next came a process called planking in which the batts were put in a bath consisting of wine waste and hot water. The felts were agitated by hand or with stirring planks. When this step was complete, the batts were stretched over wooden molds and shaped into hats of desired sizes. They were shaped by rubbing them with a pumice stone to produce a smooth surface, brimmed, and sent to be dyed. Near the end of the process, a stiffening agent was applied, and steam was used to seal the felt and create the final shape. An unfortunate side effect was that the steam freed traces of mercury used earlier in the process, and the resulting mercury vapor is what seems to have been most responsible for the nerve and brain damage causing Mad Hatter

Syndrome (Feinstein).

The part of hat-making involving mercury was quite dangerous. Workers exposed to the mercury vapor developed symptoms of mercury poisoning, which can be severe. The phrase "Mad as a Hatter" comes from the severe behavioral and physiological symptoms exhibited by hat makers who were exposed to mercury poisoning (Van Patten).

Beaver hats first appeared in Europe in the late Middle Ages. They were made in Flanders, and later, Spain and France. They were very expensive. The beaver pelts from which the hats were made came from the Eurasian beaver from Scandinavia and Russia. There probably were still some populations of beaver in Central Europe in the later Middle Ages (Chico 47). The first recorded mention of a beaver hat is in a text by no less than Geoffrey Chaucer, who wrote of a "Flaundrish bever hat" in 1386 (Wilcox 115).

Beaver pelts were used elsewhere, particularly in China, to make coats and decorate robes and other clothes; there was no Asian equivalent of the European hat trade. Beaver pelts were among the furs traded to China from the northwest coast area, as were seal skins and sea otter pelts. This trade was large, profitable, and lasted many decades, but it did not involve hats. The sea otter trade with China was what kept Russian America (mostly parts of Alaska) financially sustainable.

Over the centuries in which beaver hats were popular, there were many styles. Among the more colorful were the floppy-brimmed hats worn by the Cavaliers (during the English Civil War). The style resumed after the Restoration of Charles II in 1660, though England under Lord Protector Oliver Cromwell did not approve of the Cavalier style since it was associated with the deposed King Charles I. These hats were often worn with plumes that moved with the breeze and motion of the wearer. The Cavalier style was essentially a wide-brimmed slouch hat with plumes of long ostrich feathers, sometimes called "weeping plumes" (Wilcox 113). The plumes were fastened to the back of the hat or on the left side, which kept them from getting in the way of a sword, if the swordsman were right-handed (Wilcox 114). These floppy hats led to other styles. Tacking the brim at the sides created a distinctive hat often seen in contemporary illustrations of naval officers, and fastening the brim on three sides created the famous tricorn hat worn during the American Revolution and common in the Napoleonic Wars.

English and French dandies were not the only groups whose hats featured feathers. An English traveler to the Ottoman lands in the 1500s remarked that the feared and famous Janissaries also wore plumes (Doughty 10). The Janissaries originated as boys given to the Ottoman authorities by Christian families in the Balkans as a kind of tax, who were converted to Islam and trained as soldiers. Because they were not from powerful Ottoman families, they were loyal only to the Sultan. Plumed hats were a part of their uniform. Other Muslim warrior groups also wore plumes, such as the Mamluks in Egypt, and both Mamluks and Janissaries were feared on the battlefield.

Birds in England and Europe did not possess plumes of the necessary size and properties, so fancy plumes were an item of international trade. Ostrich plumes would have come from Africa by one of several trade routes involving Muslim traders. This early plume trade may have driven ostriches in North Africa to extinction.

In 1604, the English king allowed London's felt makers to incorporate, which facilitated the development of hat making in England. The incorporation was intended to build the domestic market and reduce imports from France (Wilcox 113). Protectionism characterized British economic policy, even with hats. In 1732, Parliament passed the Hat Act, which, among other things, restricted the import of hats from the English North American colonies. The colonists used cheaper grades of beaver to make hats and export them to Britain. The restrictions probably hurt, but the colonies were growing rapidly and had a sizable domestic market (Backhouse 70).

Quality beaver hats were expensive, but they lasted for years, often passing from father to son. Prices remained high during the entire fur trade period, which meant that beaver hats were generally confined to the prosperous. In the 1600s, a fine beaver hat in England cost three to four pounds sterling, which was two to three months' pay for an unskilled worker. They were also valuable enough to steal (Carlos and Lewis 23). Their value would have been enough to have a thief hanged, but more than likely, the thief would have been "transported" to the British colonies and sold as an indentured servant for a term of usually seven years.

The quality of hats varied, with the lower quality fur hats being cheaper. The felt going into a hat could be beaver wool mixed with muskrat or felt from other furs (Carlos and Lewis 16). There is no information available on hat-makers cheating, but the temptation to mix other materials in with the beaver wool when making a hat and passing it off as pure beaver must have been strong.

The price of a fine beaver hat in London in the 1770s was 21 shillings, more than twice the nine shillings weekly wages of an unskilled laborer. In New York, an 1825 newspaper advertisement depicts men's beaver hats priced from $5.00 to $8.00, with imitation beaver priced at $4.00. "Roram" hats, made of cheaper felt and coated with beaver fur, ranged from $2.00 to $3.25, and an 1825 fancy beaver hat selling for $8.00 would be priced at over $200.00 today (Holloway).

There was even some folklore involving these hats. One belief was that wearing a beaver hat would gradually make the wearer more intelligent. There was even the belief that deafness could be cured by wearing a beaver hat.

After about 1790, Britain's first postal carriers were given uniforms including standard beaver "issue hats" (Chico 47). Beaver hats were also the specified headgear of a number of British military units. Over the centuries, the styles of beaver hats changed, but beaver felt remained the prime material for fine hats on account of its durability and resistance to water. Among the styles over these years were the Wellington (1812), the Paris Beau (1815), the Dorsay (1820), and the Regent (1875).

The dominance of the beaver hat as a fashion item only truly began to change in the 1820s when silk hats began to replace them. The silk hats had bodies constructed from cotton, which was wrapped around a form and coated in shellac. Once it hardened, it was covered with silk plush and processed. The resulting hat was cheaper than beaver, and still quite durable and water repellant (Backhouse 94).

The hatting industry attracted much legislative debate in England, and, as the emerging major supplier of the world's finest furs, the Hudson's Bay Company was often at the center of discussion. Before its 1690 re-chartering, English hatters, who wanted to obtain their raw materials at the lowest prices possible, convinced parliament to place stricter rules for sales on the Company. The results were that the Company was required to have a public sale of pelts in London between two and four times a year. The sale would take place by auction, and the pelts were required to be sold in relatively small quantities, a requirement requested by the small hat makers who wanted access to the Hudson Bay furs. The pelts were sold at candle auctions, a way of setting the closing of the bids. The highest bidder at the moment a candle, lit at the outset of the auction, went out would win the lot.[7] It is a testament to the Hudson's Bay Company's almost immediate and growing importance to the fur trade that the industries of England were so quickly affected. In terms of volume, the Company produced a steady stream of desirable pelts that kept English manufacturers, as well as their competitors, busy. While much can be said about the company's decisions regarding trade post locations, commitment to quick turnaround times for ships heading to England, and the credit made available to traders who worked to make contact with Indian groups, it is the Indian groups that came to the trade posts seeking goods that delivered the actual goods that the rest of the world desired.

Much of the history concerning early trade relations with the Indians of the region relies on manufacturing records and correspondence since neither the early French traders nor Indian groups maintained written histories or records of their transactions.[8] Rather than painting the tribes who traded with the English and French simplistically as victims being cheated or taken advantage of, Carlos and Lewis focused on this correspondence to reveal the Crees, Assiniboine, Dakotas, and Chipewyans[9] as equal players in the supply and demand transactions taking place in both New France and in Rupert's Land.

Trade was not only an economic exchange, but also a social one. Native groups liked the formality and ceremony of a pre-business gift exchange. Here, the native trade leader and the governors of the post would meet outside following an announcement by initial Indian gunfire

---

[7] Carlos and Lewis, 29.
[8] Ibid., 69.
[9] Ibid., 70

and a response of cannon and flag-raising by the fort. The native leader was often presented with a suit of clothing and his fellow traders with food goods and tobacco. In return the governors would be presented with pelts. After additional ceremony, actual trade took place at the post's warehouse, where the native leader would enter for negotiations.[10] The rest of the Indian traders were to remain outside, trading through the post's windows while they waited for their leader to emerge.

The Metis people, later one of the three recognized aboriginal groups in Canada, were an Indian group that came from marriages between French traders and Indian women, but Scotch and English cultures were also heavy influencers among the Metis. The term comes from a Latin word for "to mix" and originally referred to the children of these relationships. The Metis would grow to become a major intermediary between the governors of Rupert's Land and the Indian traders with the Company, and after 1800, "considered themselves a separate nation, different from other people, including the Indians and the French."[11]

---

[10] Carlos and Lewis, 73.

[11] Peter Bakker, *A Language of Our Own: The Genesis of Michif, the Mixed Cree-French Language of the Canadian Métis* (New York: Oxford University Press, 1997), 28.

A Metis trader

As trade developed in Rupert's Land, a medium of exchange became desirable. When officers of the Company or traders met up with Indians who had furs to trade, a post was not always nearby and the goods desired by the Indians might not be in stock in that post. A system of coinage, then, was developed that would not only allow the Indians to be "paid" for their pelts immediately, but also allow them to spend the money later. The first coins were made of ivory, wood, or shell and were known as Made Beaver coins. The name came from the idea that the value of one coin corresponded with the price of a perfect adult beaver pelt, which simplified trade and relieved the load of goods that traders would need to carry on their person. Now that purchases could be made later, the pelt portion of the transaction could carry on while the natives saved their money for a convenient time to buy. So widely used were the coins that goods eventually became known as having a value in Made Beaver (MB). Brass and aluminum tokens eventually replaced the wood, shell, and ivory, and eventually, Fox coins came to replace Beaver coins. Not only did the Hudson's Bay issue coins, but their competitor, the North West Company produced its own Made Beaver coins. As with any tool that makes transactions easier and faster, the Made Beaver coins not only regulated the fur trading industry and its prices, it also provided stability for many of the tradesman who had a standard of value when conducting transactions.[12]

The fur trade had its tensions, but for many years, traders and natives worked out their own systems, times, and traditions, allowing many different groups to interact and even compete without issues that led to war. Though Indian groups sometimes found themselves in conflicts based on long-standing rivalries or relations with the Europeans, most of the fur traders, the trappers, the Indians, and Company officials lived peaceably. The great amount of distance from one another in this land of millions of miles likely helped to alleviate tensions. When a new vision for the Hudson's Bay came about, one where settlers, not itinerants, would be responsible for the colony, the rules changed.

The Pacific Northwest

In the first half of July 1776, two events took place that would radically transform the complexion of the known world. On July 4, the United States declared its independence from Britain while in the midst of the Revolution. A week later, on July 12, Captain James Cook set off from the Royal Navy Docks, Plymouth, commencing his third voyage of discovery. Commanding the HMS *Resolution* and leading the HMS *Discovery*, Cook would add the Pacific coast of North America to the growing British sphere of influence. His specific orders were to locate the Northwest Passage, which, in the late 18th century, was emerging as the Holy Grail of European navigation. Expeditions of this nature, however, tended to be opportunistic, and while the discovery of the Northwest Passage would have granted Cook a special place in the pantheon of naval explorers, it would offer little in the matter of strategic advantage. That lay in taking

---

[12]"HBC Fur Trade Tokens." Manitoba Government Archives. <http://www.gov.mb.ca>

note of and observing regions of particular value to the British Empire.

Cook

Cook was by then arguably the captain with the most intimate knowledge of the Pacific Ocean. Over the course of two previous voyages, he had charted many of the far-flung islands, as well as the significant land-masses of Terra Australis and New Zealand. This time, rounding the Cape of Good Hope, Cook struck out across the southern Indian Ocean, revisiting Australia and New Zealand before arriving on the shores of the Pacific Northwest sometime in the spring of 1778. There, he encountered the kind of "vile, thick and stinking fogges" on the coast of Oregon that Sir Francis Drake experienced some two centuries earlier. On that voyage, Drake named the country, barely visible through the mist and rain, "Nova Albion," claiming it for Britain in a rather perfunctory ceremony before heading south back to the tropics and the lucrative business of robbing Spanish targets.

After Drake's brief visit and hasty departure, the Pacific Northwest remained unvisited, except perhaps for an occasional secretive Spanish expedition north from Mexico, until Cook arrived in 1778. The Spanish, of course, had a better sense of the northwest coast of America than any other European power, but they tended to keep their discoveries to themselves, so in general, the British and French were unaware of much in the way of Spanish progress. These expeditions were, in any case, superficial, and no particular discoveries were made or documented.

Cook, on the other hand, took the same methodical approach as he had on his first two voyages, and his expedition of 1778 was recognized, for the most part, as the first modern, comprehensive mapping survey. It was certainly the first to help the Europeans actually understand the region. At the time, the parts of the coast indisputably claimed by Spain lay mainly below the 40th Parallel, and Cook was instructed not to approach the western seaboard at any point lower than that. Beyond that, he was ordered merely to proceed north along the coast to a latitude of 65 degrees, and if he found the Northwest Passage, he was to sail through it, remaining alert also for a Northeast Passage across the top of Russia. He was also to take detailed notes of possible natural resources and to take possession on behalf of the Crown any territory not claimed either by France, Spain, or Russia.

Beset by foul weather, Cook failed to observe either the mouth of the Columbia River or the entry to the Strait of Juan de Fuca, the latter being the entrance to Puget South. He did, however, discover and enter Nootka Sound on the east shore of Victoria Island, which he assumed was part of the mainland. There he dropped anchor, remaining for a month or so as his ships were repaired and while he and his officers compiled a detailed report on the character of the natives and the attributes of the land upon which they lived. Oddments of equipment, blankets, and trinkets were traded, especially for sea otter pelts that were abundant on shore, and which the crew used for coats and bedding.

By May 1778, the *Resolution* and the *Discovery* had toured the Aleutian Islands, passed through the Bering Strait and entered Arctic waters. By mid-summer, the expedition arrived a point a little past 70 degrees. There the two ships ran up against a wall of ice, and after exploring it briefly and narrowly escaping being crushed, Cook realized that it could not be penetrated. With that, he set a course back to the northern Pacific.

The expedition subsequently returned south to a group of islands Cook named the "Sandwich Islands," later the Hawaiian Islands, and there the expedition passed the winter. However, Cook and five members of his crew were killed during a minor military expedition to punish the natives for stealing, which marked an unexpected end to what had been a brilliant career. The two ships, then under the command of Captain Charles Clerke, tried one more time to break through the Arctic ice, but again they failed, so they set a course homeward via the Chinese mainland. There, as they pulled in to Canton (Guangzhou) to replenish supplies, something entirely unexpected happened - the sea otter pelts that had been acquired in North America for mere trinkets sold in Canton for extraordinary sums. When they were gone, Chinese merchants clamored for more. The crew tried to persuade Captain Clerke to return to the Pacific Northwest to pick up more, which he refused to do, but if the expedition was searching for some valuable trade resource, then sea otter pelts definitely fit the bill.

Although Cook's third expedition cost him his life and failed to locate the Northwest Passage, it did succeed in putting the Pacific Northwest on the map. Before long, fur traders and explorers were probing a coast newly mapped and documented by the Admiralty, while other notable Royal Navy expeditions, in particular that of George Vancouver, were mounted to add to the general store of knowledge. It was Vancouver who explored and mapped the Puget Sound, named for his lieutenant Peter Puget. Within two decades of Cook's death, the Pacific Northwest was a known quantity.

Vancouver

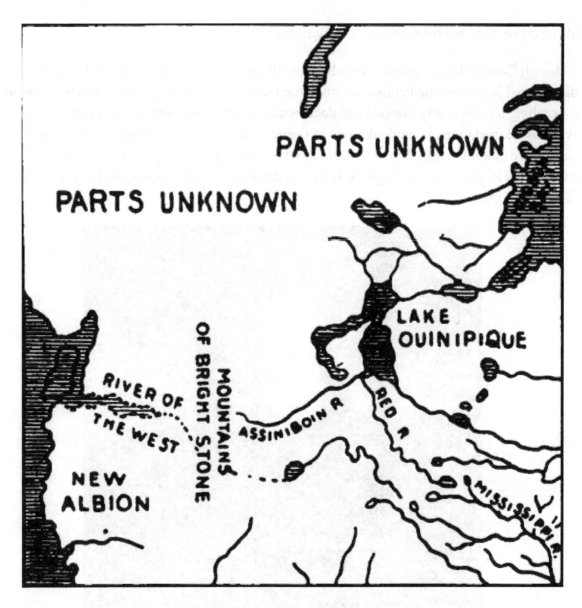

A 1778 map of the region

The Pacific Northwest was the last temperate region on the planet to yield its secrets to European knowledge, but by the 1790s, there were four significant powers present in the region, each with an expressed interest in it. The senior power was Spain, but Russia, Britain and the United States were all poised to develop interests in the region.

The Spanish were given their mandate in 1493 when a proclamation was issued by Pope Alexander VI granting any land not under a Christian ruler to Portugal and Spain. Portuguese mercantile interests at the time were focused on the coast of Africa, the Middle Passage, and the Trans-Atlantic Slave Trade, but it was Spain that left the most profound imprint in the region, even though the Spanish Empire did not devote a lot of resources to any coastal territory north of Mexico. It was from there that tropical trade routes linked Spanish territory in the New World with the Philippines and the European mainland. On behalf of England, Sir Francis Drake peered briefly into the fog, but beyond that, he continued to apply himself to plundering the Spanish, which was a far more lucrative enterprise.

What motivated the Spanish to become more proactive in the region was Russia. The impetus of Russian investment in the region adjoining the far east of Siberia was imperial on the one hand, but mercantile on the other. Their greatest interest was the region's furs, and Russian fur traders had been active along the coast of Siberia for more than a century, but it was only towards the end of the reign of Tsar Peter the Great that a concerted effort was made to explore and exploit the land farther east. The possibility that eastern Russia was linked by land to western America remained a definite possibility, and it was Peter the Great who authorized the first expeditions to investigate the general lay of the land beyond the borders of Siberia.

After Peter's death in 1725, it was his widow and successor, Catherine I, who pushed forward the quest, launching within weeks of her ascent to the throne a definitive expedition led by Vitus Bering. Bering would ultimately command two expeditions, the first of which established the existence of a strait between Siberia and Alaska. The second expedition, which was much more elaborate, crossed the Bering Strait, and in 1741 the Russians began a comprehensive and detailed scientific survey. Bering would not survive this expedition, but the Russian flag was raised on the bleak shores of Alaska, which would remain in Russia's possession for more than a century.

Like the Spanish, however, the Russians did not widely publicize their activities in Alaska and along the Pacific Northwest coast. Nonetheless, Russia's presence was enough the galvanize the Spanish, and through the 1760s and 1770s, the Spanish became conspicuously more active in the region of California, reaching as far north as the Queen Charlotte Islands in an expedition mounted in 1774. A year later, the Spanish penetrated as far north as 58 degrees, taking note on the return journey of the mouth of the Columbia River. In 1776, the year that Captain James Cook embarked from England on his final expedition, the Spanish incorporated the settlement of San Francisco, which one day would become one of the most important seaports and cities on the Pacific coast. In 1779, an expedition commanded by Ignacio de Arteaga got as far north as Mount St. Elias.[13] It was at this point that the Spanish and Russians made cautious contact.

This, at least on paper, added a vast new region of America to the Spanish Empire. As the Spanish pressed north, however, and the Russians moved south, Captain James Cook, with the audacity reserved only for a captain of the Royal Navy, made landfall precisely at the junction of these two imperial spheres of influence, poised like a wedge. Cook dropped anchor, stood on the quarterdeck, surveyed the prospects, and was perfectly willing to be the spark that would ignite a major international crisis.

---

[13] Vitus Bering in fact observed the same sight from somewhat further north.

The catalyst of all of this, apart from the imperial ambitions of all three competing powers, was the fur trade. As Cook's men discovered in Canton, the lustrous pelt of the sea otter, the finest that nature could contrive, commanded outrageous profits, and before long traders from many nations were establishing their presence in the region. With that, Nootka Sound became the most important port of call and trading entrepôt on the coast, even as its sovereignty remained unresolved. The competition was mainly between the British and Spanish, and the first Spanish mariner to observe the port, a man named Juan Pérez, did not make a formal claim on behalf of Spain. Instead, he merely recorded a brief description of what he had seen. Cook also made no formal claim, simply because he assumed that the Spanish already had.

By the end of the 1780s, therefore, the Spanish were confident that annexation of the coast up to the point of contact with the Russians was secure. However, mainly because of the fortunes to be made in the fur trade, the British were now apt to challenge them, and the United States, anxious to develop new markets after its separation from Britain, also began to show an interest.

In the summer of 1789, Spain launched an aggressive expedition to occupy Nootka Sound, which immediately outraged British traders and prompted a diplomatic standoff between the two powers. A British merchant ship under the command of Captain James Colnett arrived in the Sound soon afterwards and was promptly seized by the Spanish, after which the British crew was sent to Mexico as prisoners. This was an extremely provocative move, and it placed the two sides near the brink of war. The crisis even engulfed the United States, which feared an imminent advance by British forces in Canada against Spanish Louisiana. The crisis was so critical that it provoked the first Cabinet-level foreign policy debate to be held in the United States under the new Constitution of 1787.

In a sign of the times, the Spanish blinked first, and the British Empire, fast becoming the strongest on the planet, emerged the winner. The Spanish agreed to claim no territory not secured by treaty or immemorial possession, which was, in effect, an almost total capitulation. This was underlined even more absolutely by a Spanish agreement to pay the British compensation for damages done to British interests in Nootka, and in due course, the Spanish began a southerly retreat that would eventually concede all of the territory north of the 42nd Parallel to the United States.

By the time he came to office as the third president, Thomas Jefferson had long worried about the future of the western U.S., seeing that settlements in the Ohio Valley and lower south relied upon the Mississippi River. France's controls over the region, in his estimation, put the U.S. at a severe disadvantage. His solution proved successful beyond his wildest imagination, for Napoleon did not only sell New Orleans to the U.S, the portion that Jefferson instructed his ministers to make an offer on, but all of "New France," the entire area of Louisiana. Jefferson might have said later that his purchase of the territory "strained" but did not "break" the

Constitution, but also should have boasted that, with one stroke, he had removed one less obstacle to American expansionism.

The Louisiana Purchase encompassed all or part of 15 current U.S. states and two Canadian provinces, including Arkansas, Missouri, Iowa, Oklahoma, Kansas, Nebraska, parts of Minnesota that were west of the Mississippi River, most of North Dakota, nearly all of South Dakota, northeastern New Mexico, northern Texas, the portions of Montana, Wyoming, and Colorado east of the Continental Divide, and Louisiana west of the Mississippi River, including the city of New Orleans. (parts of this area were still claimed by Spain at the time of the Purchase.) In addition, the Purchase contained small portions of land that would eventually become part of the Canadian provinces of Alberta and Saskatchewan. The purchase, which doubled the size of the United States, still comprises around 23% of current U.S. territory.

The purchase was a vital moment in Jefferson's presidency. At the time, it faced domestic opposition as being possibly unconstitutional, and though he felt that the U.S. Constitution did not contain any provisions for acquiring territory, Jefferson decided to purchase Louisiana because he felt uneasy about France and Spain having the power to block American trade access. Jefferson also decided to allow slavery in the acquired territory, which laid the foundation for the crisis of the Union a half century later. On the other hand, Napoleon Bonaparte was looking for ways to finance his empire's expansion, and he also had geopolitical motives for the deal. Upon completion of the agreement, Bonaparte stated, "This accession of territory affirms forever the power of the United States, and I have given England a maritime rival who sooner or later will humble her pride."

The purchase also allowed Jefferson to plan something he had talked about since taking office: an expedition deep into the unmapped and largely unknown continent, with the final destination being the Pacific Ocean. Even before the Louisiana Purchase, and against the advice of those who expected that France and Spain would object, Jefferson had already planned to send Meriwether Lewis and a team through the lands claimed by France and Spain. The historical body of scholarship is united in its appraisal of how, "[t]he political climate in 1803 complicated Jefferson's request." "He had asked Congress to authorize a military reconnaissance into unknown lands that already were claimed by the two most powerful nations in the world, France and Britain, with a third, Spain, clinging to a hold in the south and far west. Jefferson already had approached Spanish officials administering the region on behalf of France, seeking their approval to pass through the Louisiana Territory for the purposes of exploration. Spanish ambassador Don Carlos Martinez objected, but Jefferson pressed ahead with his request to Congress."

With the Louisiana territory squarely in American possession, Jefferson could now embark upon his great plan. In their own way, Meriwether Lewis and William Clark could bring something to the expedition that would offset the problems Jefferson saw developing in

America's "wild west" of the late 18th and early 19th centuries. Between the Appalachians and the Mississippi, Americans rapidly filled up the land, and historians have taken note about the state of the colonists in the region: "The half-million Americans (one out of 10) who already lived west of the Appalachian Mountains, however, felt they had found their own "national" interests. Since water routes were viewed as a source of commerce, many people along the Mississippi viewed themselves as the seeds of an independent nation that would tap into the world marketplace, not by going east to the Atlantic seaboard, but by following the Ohio and Mississippi river system down to the Gulf of Mexico." [14]

Thus, Jefferson was anxious about the American settlers on the frontier who might drift away from the Republic. Kingmakers and men of destiny could prove to be the worst thing the U.S. faced, and his own vice-president (Aaron Burr) would serve as the most stunning example, but of even greater concern was the quality of American settlements in the West. Jefferson wanted to spread American civilization and Republican institutions, not merely seed the wilderness with American stock. The way to approach the problem was to enrich the fortunes of the American settlers of this new vast territory. He had meant to do that by taking control of the Mississippi and New Orleans, knowing that their fortunes lay with access to trade and the ability to sell their products.

It's hard to determine exactly what Jefferson had in mind with Native Americans, especially what he thought of their future, and perhaps what challenges they might present to an expanded Republic. However, he still had to deal with the present. "The West was not simply a blank slate during the early years of the Republic. The Indian peoples who inhabited the region constituted formidable obstacles to the progress of American settlement. But they also possessed invaluable information about the continent and its resources that Jefferson and his countrymen sought to exploit."[15]

Thus, from 1804-1806, the first expedition across the North American continent was commissioned by Jefferson and led by Lewis and Clark to traverse the continent until they reached the Pacific, studying everything from the ecology to geography along the way to get an understanding of the country's new region. In fact, Lewis and Clark would find far more than they bargained for. The 33 men who made the trip came into contact with about two dozen Native American tribes, many of whom helped the men survive the journey, and along the way they met and were assisted by the famous Sacagawea, who would become one of the expedition's most famous participants. Though they suffered deaths on their way west, the group ultimately reached the Pacific coast and got back to St. Louis in 1806, having drawn up nearly 150 maps and giving America a good idea of much of what lay west.

---

[14] "Circa 1803 (Living in America)." Lewis and Clark: The Journey of the Corps of Discovery, A Film by Ken Burns. http://www.pbs.org/lewisandclark/inside/idx_cir.html (accessed November 3, 2012).

[15] Onuf, Peter S. "Thomas Jefferson and the Expanding Union." *Lewis and Clark: Journal to Another America, edited by Alan Taylor* Missouri Historical Society Press (2003): 165

Lewis and Clark

Just by the diligent efforts of collecting samples and cataloguing their observations, the Corps of Discovery made major contributions to the field of science, particularly in determining the geography of the place. Lewis and Clark did so with the production of dozens of maps that marked "their progress and meticulously recorded geographical detail as a guide to locating sites more precisely...The result revolutionized American notions of geography in general and of the West in particular." In essence, the continent became knowable and its accuracy served the interests of national ambitions. Making accurate maps accomplished just that, especially when "Clark made it clear that there existed no easy river-and-portage route to the Pacific." In this way, the failure to locate the fabled Northwest Passage did not end the dream of a route to the riches of the "Orient," but instead replaced them with a new map, where the new "orient" had been discovered in America's West. When "Clark recognized the presence of the American Indian and - significantly - recorded it on his maps," he created a new location for riches that American settlers could aspire towards in the great westward movements of the 19th century. While "it would take many more expeditions to disabuse Americans of such ideas," the maps produced by the expedition ensured future American settlers could become the masters of the continent. Accuracy served imperial ambitions, and "Lewis and Clark had made that possible."[16]

In kind, one goal of the expedition involved the ambitions to control or at least establish relations with Native American tribes as a source of trade and commerce throughout the Mississippi Valley and the regions beyond all the way to the Pacific Ocean. "In 1808, Territorial Governor Lewis wrote a revealing treatise on 'governing the Indian nations' of the West and

---

[16] Konig, David Thomas. "Thomas Jefferson's Scientific Project and the American West." *Lewis and Clark: Journal to Another America, edited by Alan Taylor,* Missouri Historical Society Press (2003): 42-43.

conducting 'trade and intercourse with the same.' He proposed strict, even coercive, policies designed to regulate white traders through official licenses; to thwart foreign competition through government factories."[17] These were grand designs, as it went without saying that the government's attempt to regulate trade on the frontiers was ambitious. Even disregarding the tendencies of the far-flung colonists living on the periphery, the great distances across the continent proved problematic for these ambitions. No matter what the freedom-living settlers wanted, Lewis sought an officially regulated trade with Native Americans, seeing it as a formative step in the process of federal control over its imperial peripheries. Even more ambitious was his attempt to claim "full sovereignty over all aspects of life in the West."[18]

Jefferson had hoped commerce could be established by the efforts of the expedition through exploration and contact with natives, and both were established. The group discovered the best ways of passage through the terrain and established ways for future American settlers to travel from one distant point to another to trade. And of course, the expedition helped make contact with dozens of different tribes and descriptions of their similarities and differences. Lewis and Clark deserve recognition for accomplishing what Jefferson set out for them to do, "the critical first survey of distant Indian Country, and their greatest legacy was in publicizing and promoting the prospects for western profits among their fellow citizens."[19]

While America's historical memory of the expedition waned by the end of the century, the exploration made important contributions to the successive periods of expansion into the American West, contributions that can be qualified by the successes of American colonists and U.S. military conquest that came after the purchase of Louisiana. No one publicly claimed an "inheritance" won by Lewis and Clark, and there was no real proclamation of ownership over land, but there was a gradual expansion of control as white settlers pushed west. Westward movements displayed fitful starts and stops, and it would be another generation before Americans spoke about Manifest Destiny, but the Corps of Discovery did validate earlier notions of perceived American hegemony over the continent.

Astor's Ambitious Plans

At the age of 17, the German born John Jacob Astor moved to London to work for his eldest brother, George, a manufacturer of musical instruments, but just three years later, he departed for the U.S. to seek his fortune, in possession of a few flutes and $25.00. Arriving at the port of Baltimore, he soon migrated north to New York City to join his brother, Henry. In 1785, he married Sarah Cox Todd, with whom he would raise seven children. In the following year, one decade after the signing of Jefferson's Declaration of Independence, Astor established his first

---

[17] 137

[18] 137

[19] Fausz, J. Frederick. "Pacific Intentions: Lewis and Clark and the Western Fur Trade." *Lewis and Clark: Journal to Another America, edited by Alan Taylor,* Missouri Historical Society Press (2003): 135.

fur shop, often going into the wilderness himself to guarantee that it remained well stocked. Within a few years, he found his calling in the larger fur and shipping trades, aptly demonstrating an intent to go well beyond the status of a provincial merchant. Astute and pragmatic, the ambitious and at times ruthless Astor owned more than a dozen ships by the turn of the century. Not yet having reached the age of 30, he was already trading in China for tea, opium, and a number of other products not native to the American continent.

Astor

Astor's imagination concocted and perfected the vision of a multi-directional flow of trade, with products crossing the continent from New York to Oregon, where he had already purchased property by 1806. The fur products would be sent on to several eastern points. Return trips would bring all manner of exotic Asian products to eastern American and European cities. On the periphery were numerous tribes of the Pacific Northwest, furnishing Astor's company with furs in return for cheaply obtained blankets and beads. Similarly, an additional source of beaver, otter, and other fur-bearing animals was to come from Russian America (present-day Alaska) through Archangelsk (now the city of Sitka). The Russians greatly preferred American business to that of European enterprises and were particularly hopeful that Britain would be pushed out of the region due to political strife between the two countries.

Well aware of the report brought back by Lewis and Clark, and aware of the British presence in the Great Lakes region, Astor went to work by soliciting the help of New York City Mayor DeWitt Clinton. Clinton's uncle served as the Vice President to Jefferson, and therefore, he had the president's ear. Astor also maintained a good relationship with Albert Gallatin, Secretary of the Treasury for the first decade of the century.

Clinton

Gallatin

Before long, Astor was able to write freely to Jefferson, who was a famously avid correspondent. Rather than providing the president with volumes of economic forecasts and speculative ledgers, he stressed the political requirements of gaining a hold on the American West. He preyed upon Jefferson's desire for expansion and his hopes for full American coffers through trade as well. Astor reminded the president of the Lewis and Clark reports, and the two developed a vision of one company's monopoly over the fur trade in its one-sided partnership with the tribes. Its operations, supply, and trade routes were all to be kept under one sphere of influence in order to prevent a European bidding war or actual military intrusion for tribal allegiances. In such a scenario, peace on the continent was to be more easily preserved, and international partnerships were rendered unnecessary, outside of clients. For Jefferson's part, expansion and eventual annexation of the western portion of the continent would come at no public cost, taking the contested land simply through a greater degree of occupation and infusion of resident industry than that of his rivals. Astor's idea, as expressed to Jefferson, went so far as to push the British out of both the Great Lakes and the Pacific Northwest entirely. More than protecting trade, the vision offered Jefferson a greater sense of security on the borders.

The anti-British sentiment was expressed with full knowledge that British goods were needed for trade with the tribes. The only legal obstacle was the recently passed Embargo Act, which forbade the acquisition of British goods in the U.S. Britain was at war with France, and both countries habitually stopped American merchant ships to check for weapons shipments and European crewmen. The Embargo Act was Jefferson's "nonviolent resistance"[20] and an expression of insistence on American rights in the trading world. The Embargo Act was passed in 1806, but it was delayed a year until a British warship fired on and detained the American warship *Leopold*.

Despite the acquisition of a charter for Astor's new company being easily obtained from Clinton, the Act hovered over his ability to start the project. Eventually, all of his ventures, including the Southwest Fur Company and the newly created Pacific Fur Company, were placed under the umbrella of the American Fur Company in 1808. The Embargo Act was revoked in 1809 in the final days of the Jefferson administration, and Astor was prepared for immediate action. However, Monroe continued such practices as an embargo against Britain in the following years, creating the tension leading up to the War of 1812. That conflict came to carry serious consequences for the Astor/Jefferson experiment. For the time being, however, Astor had secured the president's blessing.

ATTACK AND MASSACRE OF CREW OF SHIP TONQUIN BY THE SAVAGES OF THE N.W.COAST

A depiction of the *Tonquin*

In 1810, through the Pacific Fur Company, Astor began to direct his energies at the still mostly unexploited regions accessible from the mouth of the Columbia River. This was, of course, in open defiance of British claims, but that was very much in keeping with Astor's style. Astor put up the money, and a group of American and Canadian fur traders managed affairs on the ground.

As Astor was setting up his company, relations between the British and Americans were

---

[20] *Encyclopaedia Britannica, The Embargo Act of 1807 – www.encyclopaediabritannica.co.uk*

becoming increasingly antagonistic. The imminent war, as it related to unresolved antipathies between Britain and the United States, generated deep anti-British feeling in the United States, and any man who was willing and able to challenge British domination of the fur trade could be guaranteed the enthusiastic support of both the United States political and mercantile establishment.

The founding of a company specifically to exploit the Pacific fur trade was even more likely to run afoul of the fragile Anglo-American relationship, for it would be pressing an American footprint deep into the vast and unclaimed quadrant of the continent, stretching from the 42nd Parallel to the 54th Parallel. This region, known informally as the Oregon Country, although formally unclaimed, nonetheless lay within what the British regarded as their own sphere of influence. Astor was warned that he might well stir up a hornet's nest by boldly entering this region, but to this he simply shrugged and replied that questions of sovereignty were for governments to answer, not him. His interest was strictly business.

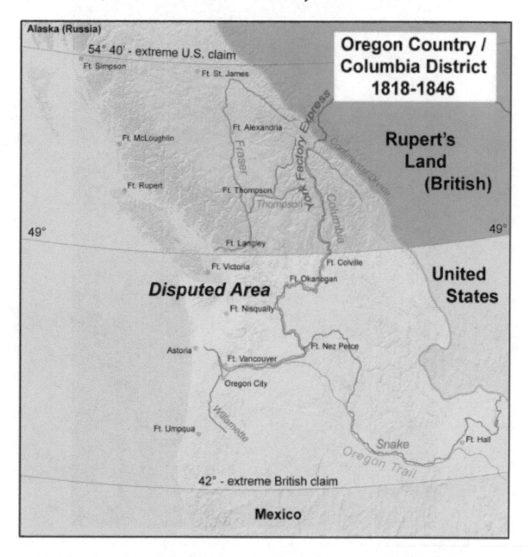

A map of the Pacific Northwest depicting the territorial claims

The overland contingent of the expedition was to be led by 27-year-old William Price Hunt, a St. Louis businessman with no particular experience when it came to this kind of expedition. Naturally, the land expedition would follow the broad course of the Lewis and Clark Expedition, setting off from St. Louis and following the upper Missouri River before crossing the continental divide into the Oregon country.

The maritime route would be led by Alexander MacKay, a Canadian fur trader and explorer, lately of the Northwest Fur Company. MacKay and Hunt were both given minor holdings in the company, as were Duncan McDougall and David and Robert Stuart.[21] These men would form the foundation of the operation, spearheading an enormously bold and ambitious venture.

---

[21] Duncan MacDougal was a Scottish born ex-clerk of the Northwest Fur Company, and the Stuart brother were Scottish born businessmen also engaged in the fur trade, and also part associates of the Northwest Fur Company.

Hunt

To establish the first trading post and facilitate the maritime expedition, Astor acquired the *Tonquin*, a three-year-old merchantman of 290-tonnes. The ship was a three-masted, square-rigged bark, armed with 12 guns and experienced in the China tea route and the Pacific timber trade. On this voyage, the ship was to be commanded by U.S. Navy Lieutenant Jonathan Thorn. Thorn was regarded as a rising star of the young U.S. Navy establishment, and at just 31 years of age, he had already seen significant action in the Tripolitan War under the command of the legendary Lieutenant Stephen Decatur. He was known for his daring and creativity under battle conditions, but his rise through the ranks, although impressive, might well have been more so had he not suffered from several well-documented defects of character. He was a bombastic, arrogant, and petulant character, impatient of command and known to be unusually fond of prescribing the lash. The cruel streak caused him to be despised by the men under his command but feared too, and he ran a highly disciplined ship, which was an attribute appreciated in a wartime navy.

**LIEUTENANT JONATHAN THORN, USN
(1779-1811)**

Thorn

The common destination of both expeditions was to be the mouth of the Columbia River. Historians have often remarked that the two commands were completely skewed, since Alexander MacKay was a man who had spent much of his life traveling and exploring in Indian country but had little or no experience as a merchant, while Hunt, whose entire life had been spent in the application of quill and ledger, had no experience whatsoever with expeditions. Hunt would certainly have performed better on the decks of the *Tonquin* and MacKay with rifle and snowshoes, but such was Astor's planning, so in the fall of 1810, each man set off pursuant to the instructions they'd been given.

The Perilous Journey to the Columbia

The *Tonquin* was towed out of New York Harbor on September 6, 1810, with 22 hands on board and 33 passengers. Let loose on the tide, a fresh northwesterly wind filled her sails, and before long she was past the busy shores of New York. Soon she was joined by the Navy frigate *Constitution* that would escort her clear of the coast. She passed Sandy Hook lighthouse on the afternoon of the following day, and by the morning of September 8, she was out of sight of land.

On a southeasterly bearing, the *Tonquin* sailed against that serene backdrop of the mid-Atlantic in the late season, but an unhappy atmosphere prevailed on board. A colossal inventory of goods, equipment, and materials had been rather haphazardly stowed, and as crew and company men, all previously unacquainted with one another, began trying to make sense of it all, tensions began to manifest.

On board was an employee of the Pacific Fur Company, a 27-year-old fur trader by the name of Alexander Ross. It was Ross who would years later publish the definitive account of the early years of the Pacific Fur Company in a book entitled *Alexander Ross's Adventures of the First Settlers on the Oregon or Columbia River*, and in it, he had this to say at the start about Lieutenant Thorn: "It was in settling this knotty point [of organization and stowage] that the crusty supremacy of the high-minded captain was first touched."

Trouble began with the assignment of ship-board accommodations to clerks of the company, who were entitled by contract to berths in second class cabins, but who were sent down to make themselves as comfortable as possible among the common sailors in communal lodgings at the lowest level of the ship. Thorn ought to have acknowledged his error once it was made known to him, but that appears not to have been in his nature. When contracts were produced and waved under his nose, he responded by assigning each clerk the additional duties of a common seaman, both by day and by night. Appeals were made to the partners, who approached the captain on behalf of their men, but this appeared to simply infuriate him more. With a finger thrust in Alexander MacKay's face, he warned the senior partner, in terms that did not invite discussion, that he would blow the brains out of any man who dared disobey his orders on board his own ship. Ross noted, "This was the first specimen we had of the captain's disposition, and it laid the foundation of a rankling hatred between the partners and himself, which ended only with the voyage, and not only that, but it soon spread like a contagion amongst all classes, so that party spirit ran high."

Thus, on the upper decks, a contest of wills began between the captains of the ship and the expedition, while on the lower decks, bets were laid on who would come out on top. In the end, the captain divided the quarterdeck, with the starboard for his men and the port for those of the company, while clerks were denied access to the quarterdeck altogether. Everyone, regardless of who they were, was ruled over with unyielding autocracy, with rules constantly shifting according to the whims of the captain and frequent toe-to-toe altercations between him and Mackay. The bad blood seemed particularly to afflict the two, and MacKay, who was 40 and thus 10 years the captain's senior, was frequently dressed down and ordered about in a manner apparently designed to cause offense, despite the fact he was the senior member on the ship.

In the meantime, the *Tonquin* sailed steadily southeast towards the coast of Africa, and while he proved himself daily to be an objectionable character, there was no doubt that Thorn was a competent captain and skilled sailor. Even as he antagonized everyone on board, he won the respect of his crew. On October 6, the *Tonquin* came in sight of Cape Verde, off the coast of West Africa, and there entered the northeasterly trade winds and began the long haul south to the coast of South America and thereafter to Cape Horn. The equator was crossed on October 25, and with all the usual ceremony, the *Tonquin* entered the southern hemisphere. On November 15, Terra del Fuego came into view, and four days later, they could see Cape Horn. Although delayed by adverse winds, the *Tonquin* rounded the Cape without mishap, and by the new year, it was northbound up the west coast of the continent. The equator was crossed again on January 24, and on February 10 the peaks of the Sandwich Islands came into view on the northern horizon.

So far, the *Tonquin* had followed the standard route around the Horn and into the South Pacific. The Sandwich Islands, or the Hawaiian Islands as they would later be known, were the established victualling point in the mid-Pacific. There, on February 13, the Tonquin dropped anchor in Kealakekua Bay, the site of Captain James Cook's death.

While anchored in this wide and scenic bay, several sailors took the opportunity to desert, which was perhaps less an indictment of Captain Thorne than the standard behavior of merchant mariners of the age, who joined and left ships frequently. Thorn, however, was a navy man, and the local people were offered a reward to hunt them down and bring them in, which they did. After a heavy flogging that was made to be a warning for everyone, Thorne addressed the ship's company. Ross described the scene, writing, "Storming and stamping on deck, the captain called up all hands; he swore, he threatened, and abused the whole ship's company, making, if possible, things worse. I really pitied the poor man, although he had brought all this trouble upon himself."

Flogging, although a standard naval punishment at the time, was not typically employed on a merchant vessel, but it certainly was not a contravention of the maritime convention. The deserters, however, were brutally flogged, and the matter was added to the long list of grievances now held against Thorn. Furthermore, a number of Hawaiian crewmen were taken on board.

Despite Thorn's warning, attempts at desertion were abundant, particularly in the South Pacific. Some succeeded, such as in the case of Jack Tar, although one Yankee was caught and confined. Welshman Emms Aymes was flogged for committing the offense, and a Mr. Johnston, an Englishman, was put in irons. Mr. Anderson, the boatswain, disappeared and was never found.

The *Tonquin* remained at anchor in the islands for three weeks, striking out into the wide Pacific once again on March 1, 1811 and steering directly for the mouth of the Columbia River. By then a sense of keen anticipation was felt as the end of a long and difficult voyage drew near. No ship of that size had yet entered the mouth of the Columbia, and no one doubted that this would be a challenging adventure.

The difficulties of personality and command were not quite yet over. The partners – MacKay, McDougall, and the Stuart brothers – had until that point made absolutely no headway in asserting their contractual command of the expedition over the captain, who had suffered a series of irritations and was obviously in no mood to compromise. The matter came to a head over the question of foul weather gear. As the ship entered the northern reaches of the Pacific, the weather began to cool, and occasional squalls and storms of sleet and snow required the distribution of warmer clothing, which in turn required disturbing the crates and bales stowed with meticulous care below. Captain Thorn, a man of compulsively ordered mind, would absolutely not permit this. It was an illogical position, of course, but the captain stuck to it and dared the partners to do what they could. A furious altercation ensued between Alexander MacKay and Captain Thorn and ended with pistols drawn. Sides were taken, and for a moment, it seemed that there would be a civil war on board the *Tonquin*. Cooler heads prevailed, eventually, when McDougall came between them and was able to calm the situation down. Captain Thorn kept his bales and boxes untouched, and the company men froze in the riggings.

On March 22, the *Tonquin* at last came in sight of land, which proved to be Cape Disappointment, an arcing promontory of land that marks the entrance to the mouth of the Columbia River. The entrance to the mouth of the river, however, was invisible, hidden behind palls of mist and rain and the uniform horizon of land and sea. Thorne was not convinced that this was, in fact, the fabled entrance to the Columbia, which is not surprising since Captain Cook, on his first passage past, missed it completely. It was only really known thanks to earlier Spanish expeditions and the landward observations of Lewis and Clark. The winter of 1805, spent at Fort Clatsop, was remarked upon by Merriweather Lewis as producing more rain than he had ever seen in his life.

The expectation on board was that the ship would return to sea or find safe harbor and wait for weather conditions to settle down, and this certainly would have been the logical course of action. However, at a point perhaps a mile offshore, Thorn ordered the first mate, a crewman named Mr. Fox, to row out in a small boat to investigate. To assist him, Thorne assigned an old French sailor somewhat past his prime and three Canadian youths who were not seamen. Two were dock workers from Lachine, the headquarter of the Hudson Bay Company in Montreal, and the other was a barber.

This was yet another illogical position to take, and initially it was met by everyone with absolute incredulity. In the distance, a line of surf was clear to see, and under storm conditions, 15-20 foot waves were protecting the mouth of the river. It would be nothing less than suicidal to venture out under such conditions in a small boat with an inexperienced crew.

There are many versions of what happened next, but it seems that Fox, about which very little is known other than that he was an experienced seaman, remonstrated bitterly and sought the support of the Pacific Fur Company partners, who backed him in the assessment that such an order was a death sentence. Thorn's response, when approached by a small deputation, was simply to repeat his order and remark, "Mr. Fox, if you are afraid of water, you should have remained in Boston."

Upon that, at about 1:00 p.m., the smaller of the ship's whaleboats was detached and lowered into the water. Fox and his men were ordered in but hesitated, and the "Astorians," as they were described, once again tried to talk sense into Captain Thorn, urging repeatedly that the ship ride out the storm elsewhere or remain at anchor until there was an improvement in the weather. This was the sensible and obvious course of action, but by then, Thorn may have sensed a conspiracy afoot. Either way, the more they urged him, the more Thorn dug in his heels.

Most of the accounts that survive of this moment paint the scene like something out of *Treasure Island*, featuring Thorn as a demonic Captain Flint. The events, however, were very real, and it is, if nothing else, a testimony to the kind of ironclad command that a navy captain enjoyed over his ship and crew that the order was obeyed. Fox's parting words, according to Alexander Ross, were, "Farewell, my friends! We will perhaps meet again in the next world."

With that, the five men set off under oars, but almost immediately they lost control. Broaching broadside on to the breakers, they were sucked towards the shore, and before covering 100 yards, a distress flag was raised, Crew and passengers mobbed the captain, pleading with him to send out a better equipped rescue. According to Ross, from whose account most other versions of the story are drawn, Captain Thorn would consider no such thing, and as the whaleboat was gradually lost to sight, he remained attached to the quarterdeck. For the next 10 minutes, he stared grimly until ordering the anchors raised and having the ship turned back out to sea.

Another version of the same story is contained in a book published in 1891, entitled *An Illustrated History of the State of Washington*, written by Reverend HK Hines. In this work, the author wrote that a second boat was sent out the next day, this time including Hawaiian outrigger experts, but after striking out a few hundred yards, it returned, having made no serious attempt to cross the bar and reporting no sign of Fox and his crew. The day after that, Thorn anchored the Tonquin in 14 fathoms of water and perhaps a mile from the breakers, and from there he allowed MacKay, Ross, David Stewart, and a number of experienced sailors to try their luck in a more substantial boat, but it too was soon stopped, and then driven back by heavy surf.

In that boat was the First Officer, whose name was Mumford. Mumford seemed to attract the particular ire of the captain, and once out of earshot, Mumford confided in the Astorians that Fox had been sent out with an inexperienced crew in an inadequate boat because Thorn wished Fox dead. His theory of why this was so was simply that Fox was an amiable and charming man who enjoyed the affections of everyone on board, and whose command of his men was achieved without violence or coercion. Thorn found that unbearable, and for no better reason than spite, he sent the men to their certain deaths.

By the time that work was published, any scurrilous theory about Captain Thorn was eminently believable, and indeed, from the pages of every history of the *Tonquin* and every episode of the history of the Pacific Fur Company, Captain Thorn emerged as the very worst kind of 19th century sea captain: tyrannical, wasteful of the lives of his crew, and arrogant to the point of psychosis. Nonetheless, he remained utterly determined, even under conditions of atrocious weather, to find a way through. Mumford was sent out again, and this time managed to sound two and a half fathoms, about six feet, before retreating.[22] Then, the third mate, by the name of Aikens, was sent out to try his luck further north, and there he was able to sound three and a half fathoms, which is about nine feet. It was at that point that Thorn considered worth trying, and the plan he proposed was simply for the boat to take continuous soundings and flag the results while the *Tonquin* would follow under shortened sail. When the channel was located, the coxswain was to fire a single shot from a pistol and then immediately return to the ship. This was done, but on the return, the boat was broached broadside by a wave estimated at 20 feet high and was quickly carried away.

Thorn, ignoring the fate of the boat crew, seized the moment and guided the Tonquin into the shallow water, scraping the hull against rocks and driving it over the sandbar, but nonetheless timing the tidal surge perfectly. As a result, the *Tonquin* broke through, and by nightfall the captain brought the boat to rest in seven fathoms of water in Bakers Bay in the lee of Cape Disappointment.

Once again, there are several versions of how this maneuver was regarded by those who observed it. There can be no doubt that Captain Thorn executed a daring but masterful movement that succeeded against the odds. No matter how much they despised the man, the partners were

---

[22] Aikens in elsewhere described as 'An old tar who had signed on to command the disassembled schooner aboard the Tonquin.' The 'schooner' was a smaller ship for coastal and estuary work stowed in the holds of the Tonquin.

forced to admit that it was a display of virtuoso seamanship. This risk, however, was enormous, and for that the general consensus was that Thorn's behavior was growing increasingly irrational and was now bordering the dangerous. Without a pilot, accurate soundings, or any maps or charts to guide a course, the outcome could easily have been very different.

The task had been accomplished, but two more lives had been lost, with only three survivors reaching shore after the sounding boat was swamped. A search was mounted for some distance in both directions, but no sign was found of the boat and crew under the command of Mr. Fox. In all, 8 lives were lost in the operation to get the *Tonquin* past the bar and into the mouth of the Columbia River. It was a poor omen for the commencement of such a bold endeavor, but perhaps more importantly, it was the clearest indication yet of the character of Captain Thorn.

Alexander Ross summed it up when writing about the costly episode of entering the Columbia: "Captain Thorn was an able and expert seaman; but, unfortunately, his treatment of the people under his command was strongly tinctured with cruelty and despotism. He delighted in ruling with a rod of iron; his officers were treated with harshness, his sailors with cruelty, and every one else was regarded by him with contempt."

The site chosen to establish a trading post was on the south side of the Columbia, 12 miles upstream of the mouth and more or less at the location of the estuary port of Astoria as it stands today. Work commenced on April 12, 1811, with workers unloading supplies, ferrying them to shore, and establishing a preliminary camp. The natives in the area were comprised primarily of Clatsop and Chinook, and they were by then well-acquainted with trade, so they knew exactly what the newcomers would value. Some brought the highly prized sea otter skins to trade, while others simply lined the shore to watch.

Captain Thorn noted with visceral disgust Duncan McDougall's immediate interest in the native women. In fact, according to McDougall's biographer, Herbert Howe Bancroft, it was not long before McDougall took a "wife" from among the local Chinook Chief Comcomly's daughters. Thorn was further enraged when MacDougall went so far as to invite the chief and his many wives on board to inspect the *Tonquin*. This, according to one of the partners, "stirred the spleen of the captain, who had a sovereign contempt for the one-eyed chieftain and all his crew."

The Battle of Woody Point

More than anything, Thorn was anxious to jettison the land-based contingent to get on with their business of building the fort while he got on with his. His business now was to explore the fur trade up the entire Oregon coast, and he was agitating to get started. A shed was constructed on the shore of Baker's Bay, and there the supplies were stowed. The rain continued throughout the operation, but trees were felled, scaffolds were built, and goods and livestock were landed. A 20 x 62 foot warehouse was constructed, as was a rough residence of barked logs. Onshore, the keel was laid, and workers assembled a trading schooner out of materials pulled up in crates from the holds of the *Tonquin*.

Once this was all complete, and under some milder weather, the *Tonquin* made for the open seas, clearing the bar this time with little difficulty. On board were Alexander MacKay, various other company employees, and an English-speaking Chehalem native by the name of Lamanse, as interpreter to the tribes of the northwest coast.[23] Once on the open water, the Tonquin set a course for Vancouver Island.

As Herbert Bancroft put it, "Our sturdy captain might now shake from his feet the dust of Scotch fur traders and filthy French voyageurs and on the Tonquin's cleanly scrubbed deck, laugh at the discordant past, laugh as with his own crew only on board she flew before the breeze, and swept gayly into the coves and estuaries of the admiring savages. Alas no, with his evil temper, evil times forever attended him. Doomed to destruction, the gods had long since made him mad."

Onshore, in the meantime, the business of felling trees and clearing ground went on. The first contacts with the natives of the district were cautious, but amiable. The schooner, *Dolly,* was quickly assembled, but at 30 tons, it was suitable only for navigating the river. Henceforth, it was envisioned that the *Tonquin* would remain offshore; having survived the entry into the mouth of the river once, there was no reason why the ship should attempt the same maneuver again.

As the *Tonquin* disappeared over the northern horizon, the managers at the fort continued with the construction, and with the essentials established, they began to explore outward and establish cordial relations with the natives to begin the business of trading for furs.

Under specific instructions from Astor, the *Tonquin* was scheduled to coast northwards for Vancouver Island, and in particular Nootka Sound, a series of deep fjords and inlets on the west shore of Vancouver Island. Thereafter, the *Tonquin* was to return to New York, laden with her priceless cargo, after briefly visiting the settlement of Fort Astoria. This was, in the future, to be the pattern, with the addition of the Chinese port of Canton.

Nootka Sound was a region with a history. On his cruise up the Pacific coast of North America in 1778, Captain Cook, having missed the mouth of the Columbia River in heavy weather, as well as the entrance to Puget South known as the Strait of Juan de Fuca, entered a deep inlet on what he assumed was the mainland. He was unaware then that it was, in fact, the western lee of a massive island, later to bear the name of George Vancouver, then an officer aboard Cook's second ship, HMS *Discovery.*

Cook, however, was not the first European to enter this deep, natural harbor, nor the first to make contact with coastal people inhabiting the idyllic shores. Four years earlier, Spanish mariner Juan Pérez entered the same sound and traded oddments of metal tools and beads for sea

---

[23] Alternatives to this name of this man are Lemazee, George Ramsey, and more recently Joseachal.

otter robes that were a characteristic garment and utility of the coastal natives.

Cook, when he arrived in 1778, anchored in the sound and spent several weeks refitting and repairing his ships. To pass the time, his officers compiled the first detailed description of the Indian tribes of the coast. They too were attracted to the brilliant sea otter pelts, and not at that time guessing their real value, purchased quite a number for whatever trinkets or metal tools they had on board. From there the *Resolution* and the *Discovery* returned south to the Sandwich Islands, where Cook lost his life at the hands of the island natives. His ships returned via China, where their officers and crew were astonished at the prices fetched for the sea otter pelts that they had so casually purchased on the shore of Vancouver Island.

Captain Cook had not left the British imprint very deep on the Pacific shore of North America, but that journey served as a training school for others who would follow, like George Vancouver. Vancouver was a young officer aboard the *Discovery*, and in the decade to follow, he would be responsible for the first comprehensive survey expedition to map and understand the complex coastline above the line of the Columbia mouth. On board that expedition was another officer destined to be immortalized by geography, Lieutenant Peter Puget, after whom the iconic Puget Sound is named.

The realization that astronomical profits were there to be made prompted other visits to Nootka Sound, and the trade in sea otter pelts began. During the remainder of the 1700s, trade in this little enclave was brisk, which in turn prompted the first questions of European sovereignty. As the senior imperial power, Spain certainly held the primary claim, but even though Juan Pérez had visited the sound four years before Cook, no written accounts were ever published. Cook, when he arrived in 1778, did not lay formal British claim to the region because he assumed that the Spanish already had. The Russians were present to the north, but they did not express any particular interest in the territory further south than the modern Alaskan panhandle.

The focus of all of this international interest was a broken coastline of rare beauty, populated by a minor collection of tribes of the Wakashan language group, and where the coveted sea otters bred and proliferated in commercial quantities. Then, sometime in mid-1789, the Spanish grasped the nettle, and an expedition sailed into the sound, and formally hoisted the Spanish imperial standard. Soon afterwards a British trading vessel under the command of Captain James Colnett entered the Nootka Sound, unaware of the Spanish claim, and began constructing a trading post. The Spanish seized the ship and arrested Colnett and all of his crew, sending them south to Mexico as prisoners.

The effect of this minor skirmish on the outer marches of the known world almost engulfed the British and Spanish empires in war. Even the United States, led by President George Washington, mobilized against the possibility that the British might take the opportunity to seize Spanish Louisiana. As historians have since observed, the Nootka Sound Crisis provoked the first cabinet-level foreign policy debate in the United States under the Constitution of 1887.

In the end, it was the Spanish who blinked first, signing a convention that was pushed under their nose by the upstart British Empire, which, despite the loss of the United States, was beginning to emerge as the premier global power of the age. Spain agreed to limit its foreign claims to those secured either by treaty or immemorial possession, as well as compensate the British for damages done to them at Nootka.

This was the situation as the *Tonquin* headed for the area. As a strictly commercial venture, and the first substantive American effort to engage in the lucrative northwest fur trade, this expedition nonetheless represented an American stake in the region. Astor, of course, had no particular interest in imperial politics, but those who did certainly had an interest in Astor's success or failure. Several nations would duke it out for sovereignty over Oregon Country, and the establishment of Fort Astoria and Captain Jonathan Thorn's minor trade expedition to Vancouver Island was the beginning for the American side.

As his anchorage, Captain Thorn chose a quiet inlet known to the natives as *Clayoquot*, or *Kyuquot*. This was an Anglicization of the Nuu-chah-nulth language name *Tla-o-qui-aht,* and it was located somewhat to the north of Nootka Sound, in the vicinity of a large native village. Lamanse warned Thorn that the inhabitants of this particular village were not to be trusted, but typically, Thorn was generally disdainful of advice, especially any advice offered by an Indian.

The *Tonquin* arrived in the bay early in the afternoon on or around June 13, 1811, and before long a small flotilla of canoes detached from the shore, laden with sea otter hides. Coming alongside, they were invited on board. Among the visitors were representatives of the chief of the village, whose name was Wickaninnish of the *Tla-o-qui-aht*. The visitors were invited to land and call on the chief's lodge, which Captain Thorn declined, but which Alexander MacKay accepted.

Lamanse again warned MacKay the Tla-o-qui-aht were not to be trusted, but he accompanied MacKay and his companions to shore, and both were hospitably received in the end. Six of Wickaninnish's men remained on board ship, however, as what historian Washington Irving described as "hostages."[24] According to Irving, "He [MacKay] was received with great professions of friendship, entertained hospitably, and a couch of sea otter skins was prepared for him in the dwelling of the chieftain, where he was prevailed upon to pass the night."

The next morning, believed to be June 14, Captain Thorn, without waiting for Alexander MacKay's return, arranged the trade goods on deck, comprising the usual selection of blankets, various types of cloth, beads, fishhooks, and various iron tools and implements, including knives and axes. With typical promptitude, he anticipated a speedy and profitable transaction, but found instead, to his irritation, that the natives were coy and apparently disinterested. Familiar with the

---

[24] Washington Irving was an American essayist and short story writer who is probably best known for his short story 'Rip van Winkle', and his 1836 publication Astoria became the basis of many subsequent accounts of the fate of the Tonquin, although it was generally regarded as a colorful and entertaining account that was at best unreliable.

fur trade, the natives were inclined to the traditional model of barter, in which negotiations and bargaining were as crucial to the process as the actual exchange.

The bargaining was led by an elderly sub-chief named Nookamis, who could recall the New England skippers and the agents of King George III. He was in no hurry to conclude any deals. Needless to say, this greatly annoyed Thorn, who Irving described as "a plain, straightforward sailor, who never had two minds, nor two prices in his dealings, was deficient in patience and pliancy, and totally wanting in the chicanery of traffic."

The process began, and when Thorn pointed at an otter pelt and then at what he was prepared to give for it, it prompted a murmur of derision and a counteroffer of precisely double. This immediately offended Thorn, who left the negotiation and paced the deck with his hands thrust into his pockets and jaw clenched in sullen silence. He was followed by the old chief, pressing the pelt in his face and crooning his counteroffer, and urging the captain to trade. This simply irritated Thorn even more, and without any better ideas, Nookamis began to loudly belittle the captain, ridiculing the mean prices that he offered. This prompted the audience to erupt in laughter. This was more than Thorn, who had likely never heard his sense of humor complimented, could bear. Irving wrote that after "turning suddenly upon his persecutor, [Thorn] snatched the proffered otter skin from his hands, rubbed it in his face, and dismissed him over the side with no very commentary application to accelerate his exit."

After applying his boot to the rear end of the dignified native and pitching him overboard in an undignified heap, Thorn then kicked the piled sea otter pelts to the left and right, scattering them across the deck and under the astonished but silent watch of his men and the assembled audience of natives. The market was broken up and Thorn disappeared into his cabin.

It goes without saying that nothing of the sort had ever happened before, and while Nookamis settled into a canoe and returned to shore with as much dignity as he could muster, one of Wickaninnish's sons, Shewish, a man in his late 30s, let it be known as he departed the ship that the insult would be answered. Gathering up their furs, the Indians abandoned the ship and set off back to shore.

When MacKay was finally able to make his way back to the ship and was told what had happened, he could hardly believe his ears. The story was relayed to him by Lamanse, who then urged MacKay to speak to Thorn in an attempt to persuade him to weigh anchor immediately and leave the vicinity. The Tla-o-qui-aht, he said, would not likely let something like that pass, and MacKay, who had his own long experience of the fur trade to draw on, was inclined to agree.

MacKay approached Thorn, who was not at that moment in a mood to be approached, and reprimanded Thorn both openly and severely for an act of crass and dangerous stupidity. In response, the captain sneered, pointed at the cannon and the small-arms locker, and asked MacKay precisely what he imagined the natives could do about it. He asked MacKay, "Do you think I would run before a lot of naked redskins so long as I had a knife or a handspike?" Shot and powder, he added as he walked away, were ample protection against an army of those he deemed savages, so the ship would remain exactly where it was. The day passed with no signs of activity or hostility on shore, which undoubtedly comforted Thorn and made him believe everything was fine. That night, he retired to his cabin at his usual time, taking no more than the usual precautions.

MacKay, however, had spent the evening in the company of those natives. In addition to the courteous treatment he had received, he had plenty of experience with other native groups' lives and cultures, and he understood quite clearly that an insult of such gravity would bring retaliation. To him, the silence on shore was ominous, and he retired that evening deeply troubled.

Historians have since conjectured that had Alexander MacKay returned to the village with the interpreter and used the good impression he had received and given the night before to try and smooth things over, it might have worked. That said, it would certainly have been a very risky strategy, and it could well have resulted in his death. It is also probable that Thorn would have been required to offer some sort of token of apology, and it can be taken for granted that he would have done no such thing.

That night, a single officer of the watch was placed on duty, but nothing was reported. Across the expanse of water, the lights of campfires remained visible deep into the night, but besides that, there was no disturbance at all.

At dawn the next morning, before Captain Thorn and Alexander MacKay were awake, a large canoe appeared alongside the ship carrying about 20 men, led by Shewish and piled high with otter pelts. Peering over the side, the crew was met by friendly faces, suggesting the Indians had forgotten all about the events of the day before and again wished to trade. Everything appeared to be normal, and since what was described as "the caution enjoined by Mr. Astor, in respect of the admission of Indians on board ship" had never really been applied, the officer of the watch allowed them to come on board.

Hearing the commotion, the captain was roused and came on deck, followed soon afterwards by Alexander MacKay, and for all appearances, the market that had been interrupted the day before was resumed. This time, however, there was little or no haggling over prices or ponderous negotiations, and Captain Thorn caught MacKay's eye and gave him a jaunty wink. In a mood of vindication, he strolled across the deck, his hands clasped behind his back, and casually observed the transactions. Soon enough, another boatload of men arrived, also laden with sea otter pelts, then a third, a fourth, and a fifth, each in turn bringing more men who clambered on board with their wares. Before long, the deck was crowded with Indians.

As more natives got on board, a sharp-eyed officer of the watch noticed that they were dressed differently than they had been the day before. They wore heavy capes, as if concealing something. He also noticed that the women remained on board the canoes, holding them steady and making no effort to come on board. A glimpse of a blade seemed to confirm that something out of the ordinary was afoot, and he immediately communicated his suspicions to MacKay, who in turn approached the captain and urged him to clear the decks immediately and set sail.

Thorn's initial instinct was to dismiss this advice, but it then seemed to dawn on him that MacKay might perhaps be right. The deck was indeed swarming with natives, and as more canoes crept alongside the ship, more climbed aboard and more still were breaking away from shore. Now somewhat alarmed, the captain assessed the situation and realized suddenly their deep peril. If the natives were armed and marshalling for an attack, then they were already outnumbered. It was too late to prime the cannon, and certainly too late to distribute small arms. Quietly, he ordered some crew members to weigh anchor, and others to climb aloft and make sail.

It then occurred to both men that the main item of trade that the Indians appeared to be interested in were knives and axes, and while the market was underway, the company traders, still oblivious to the threat, were handing out the very weapons that could be used against them, at prices that they could hardly believe. As each Indian was handed a weapon, he moved away, making room for another, and by degrees, they were distributed across the deck, all now armed.

The anchor, in the meantime, was halfway up and sails were unfurling when the captain abruptly ordered the decks cleared. As he did, a signal cry went up, probably from Shewish, which was taken up all over the ship. Knives and axes were brandished, war clubs slipped out from under garments, and each native began attacking a predetermined target.

The first to be struck was James Lewis, Alexander MacKay's clerk, who was leaning on a bundle of furs watching the trading before having a knife plunged into his back. MacKay was set upon by several attackers, and in the struggle, he was pitched overboard, landing in the water in the midst of the canoes. There he was immediately swarmed by women who clubbed him to death as he struggled in the water. Captain Thorn, armed only with a clasp knife and showing considerable mettle, set upon Shewish and apparently killed him before he was beaten down by clubs and tossed overboard. Irving claimed that Thorn killed many more than just one native, writing, "The captain had barely time to draw his clasp knife, with one blow of which he laid the young savage dead at his feet. Several of the stoutest followers of Shewish now set upon him. He defended himself vigorously, dealing crippling blows to right and left, and strewing the quarter-deck with the slain and wounded."

While the details of Irving's account all need to be taken with a pinch of salt, he went on to describe Thorn fighting his way towards the cabin where the firearms were stored, which would have been an obvious direction, but by the time he reached the wheel, he was covered with deep gashes and bleeding profusely. There he was smashed in the back of the head with a war club, after which he went down. Fighting alongside him was James Thorn, the captain's younger brother, who was serving as a ship's boy. He too was killed soon after.

By then, the surviving crew members rallied somewhat and were fighting with knives, clubs, and handspikes, but quickly they were overpowered and either clubbed or hacked to death. Seven crew had been sent aloft to release the sails, and from the rigging, they watched the carnage taking place below in horror. One was the armorer, Stephen Weekes. Without weapons of any sort, the men let themselves down by the running rigging in an effort to get below deck. One fell and was instantly killed, and another received a heavy blow with a battle axe in the back and was killed immediately as he stumbled and fell. Weekes was badly wounded, but he and three others were able to make it the cabin, where they barricaded the door and then smashed open the gun locker. A handful of muskets were loaded, and on the main deck, they fired volleys into the group of Indians now crowding the deck and already starting to loot the dead bodies.

This tended to even things out somewhat, and as the attackers began to drop dead in ones and twos, the remainder scrambled over the side of the ship, taking to their canoes with their loot and heading back to shore. The four crewmen then primed the light shipboard cannon and laid down a curtain of grapeshot, which, according to Irving, "did great execution among the canoes, and drove all the savages to shore."

Lamanse, upon whose eyewitness testimony every account of this battle is based, took no part in it, and he was spared by the attackers for the probable reason that he was one of their own. In the confusion of the retreat, he found himself on board one of the canoes and was swept back to shore along with the others. Several volleys of grapeshot laid into the retreating flotilla must certainly have done considerable damage, and no doubt many lives were lost, but Lamanse survived.

The entire melee had lasted no more than a few minutes, during which Thorn, MacKay, and 24 crewmen, half of them Hawaiians, were killed. Only four men survived. For the remainder of the day, nothing more happened, and one can suppose that in an effort to clean up and make sense of what had taken place, the bodies were thrown overboard, where they floated about the ship's keel.

For the survivors, the situation was obviously desperate. Weekes, although still alive, was obviously dying, and it was perhaps he who suggested that the three able seamen leave in a whaleboat under cover of darkness and try and make good their escape down the coast and back to Fort Astoria. This was agreed to, since inevitably they would die on board if they remained. That evening, as darkness fell, a boat was lowered over the side, and the three carefully piloted it through the sound in the direction of the open water.

As dawn rose the next morning, a handful of canoes detached themselves from the shore and carefully approached the ship to investigate. On board one of them was Lamanse, who recognized the surviving crewman, possibly Weekes, who survived the night, but who certainly was unlikely to survive much longer. He communicated to Lamanse the fact that he was alone on board and disappeared below as the first Indians began to clamber aboard. Once on the deck, they immediately set about looting the ship.

The surviving crewman, in the meantime, was forgotten as it was communicated to shore that all was clear. An armada of canoes detached from the village, and before long the deck of the *Tonquin* was swarming with Indians, who broke into the holds and began to distribute a bonanza of trade goods. Down below, however, the last survivor locked himself in the powder magazine, and there he listened to the pounding of feet above him and the whoops of joy and smashing of doors as the Indians made their way from deck to deck. Judging the moment, and before his strength deserted him, he lit a line of powder, and within seconds the ship erupted into a ball of flame.[25]

The ensuing explosion completely destroyed the ship and killed almost everyone on board. Lamanse, however, who was standing on the main chains, survived by being blown into the water, sustaining only minor injuries. He was able to make it to shore in a canoe as debris and body parts rained down for hundreds of yards in every direction. Irving wrote, "According to [Lamanse's] statement, the bay presented an awful spectacle after the catastrophe. The ship had disappeared, but the bay was covered with fragments of the wreck, with shattered canoes, and Indians swimming for their lives, or struggling in the agonies of death, while those who had escaped the danger remained aghast and stupefied or made with frantic panic for the shore."

According to Lamanse, over 100 Indians were killed in the initial explosions, and probably twice that number were maimed and injured. For weeks afterwards, the remains washed up on shore. In the immediate aftermath, the village was in utter consternation. Irving noted, "The warriors sat mute and mournful, while the women filled the air with loud lamentations."

That evening, in the midst of all the shock and grief, the three unfortunate crewmen who had attempted an escape were led into the village. Having crept out of the sound under cover of darkness, they were unable to push past the line of breakers covering the inlet, and setting boat on shore, they were attempting to manhandle it past the line of surf when they were captured by men of the Nuu-chah-nulth, a neighboring tribe, and returned to village. Irving was no doubt correct when he wrote of them, "Better had it been for those unfortunate men had they remained with Lewis, and shared his heroic death: as it was they perished in a more painful and protracted manner, being sacrificed by the natives to the manes of their friends with all the lingering tortures of savage cruelty."

There are no specific details on how the last three men met their end, but bearing in mind the preceding events, there would have been a great deal of anger and grief to add to the usual

---

[25] The fact that the powder magazine was blown tends to lend credibility to the claim that the last surviving crew member was Weekes, who was the armorer, and would have been better equipped to do this.

motivation for inflicting torture and death on captured enemies, which was, among many tribes, a standard ritual. As far as Lamanse was concerned, he remained in the village for some time as a sort of prisoner at large. Upon escaping eventually, he made his way back to the lower Columbia, where the news of the fate of the *Tonquin* was communicated to the residents of Fort Astoria.

The battle, such as it was, came to be known as the Battle of Woody Point. Although no such place exists on the map of Vancouver Island today, Cook named a particular promontory "Woody Point," which is now called Cape Cook or Brooks Peninsular. The battle took place within sight of that spot.

The End of Fort Astoria

It was at least two months before the first snippets of news of the battle began to drift south, arriving at Fort Astoria via a group of wandering Indians originating on the north shore of the Strait of Juan de Fuca. At first, the news, amounting to no more than a rumor, was met with caution, but as other nomadic coastal tribes passed by, the rumor was gradually substantiated and then confirmed by the interpreter Lamanse when he finally appeared back in Fort Astoria after his escape.

The news placed the residents of the settlement in a very grave situation, and until Lamanse appeared back at the fort, the true cause of the disaster was not understood. As such, it was sensed that the destruction of the *Tonquin* might be a precursor to a more general native plot to destroy the settlement. McDougall was even suspicious of the local Chinook and their one-eyed Chief Comcomly, who was soon to be his father-in-law. Comcomly, of course, was entirely innocent, but taking no chances, MacDougall ordered the construction of fortifications in preparation for an attack. The fort was now entirely cut off from the outside world, without any prospect of communication with New York, and months shy of any kind of reinforcement from the overland party.

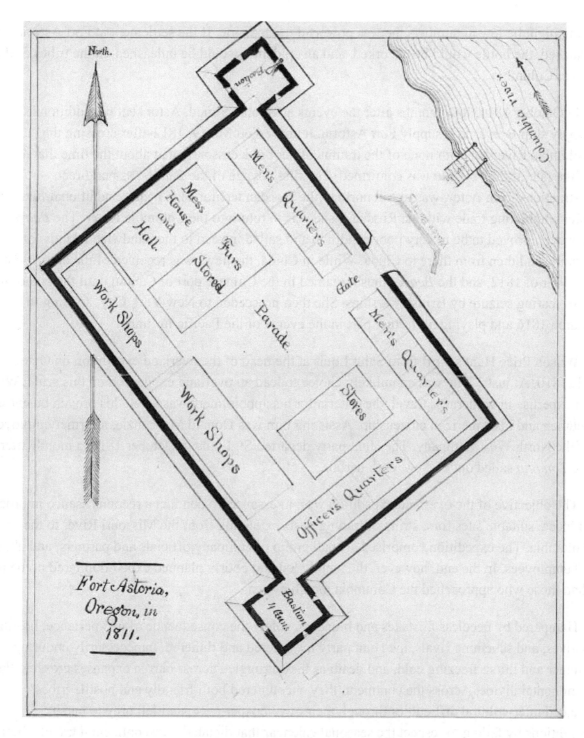

An 1811 model of the fort's layout

Showing remarkable ingenuity, however, McDougall devised a scheme that would play on both the superstition of the local tribes and the widespread fear of smallpox, which had, since the first arrival of whites on the shores of the Pacific Northwest, wrought havoc on the native population. McDougall called a meeting of all the local chiefs, and presenting them with a corked glass bottle, he declared that therein was held the smallpox medicine, and while the white man might be few in numbers, he was powerful in medicine. If the settlement at Fort Astoria was attacked, the bottle would be uncorked, and an epidemic would be unleashed on the tribes of the lower Columbia.

In October 1811, four months after the events at Nootka Sound, Astor sent the additional supply ship *Beaver* to resupply Fort Astoria. It arrived on May 9, 1812 after crossing the Columbia River bar with none of the trauma of her predecessor, and at about the time that news of the fate of the *Tonquin* was confirmed. The first voyage of the *Beaver*, as per direct instructions from Astor, was to sail north to the Russian territories to acquire additional furs, and after completing trade with the Russians, she was to return to the Columbia River. The *Beaver*, however, proved to be in very poor condition and sailed instead to the Sandwich Islands for repairs, and then from there to China. While in China, the news was received of the outbreak of the War of 1812, and the *Beaver* thus remained in the Chinese port of Canton until the end of the war, fearing seizure by British warships. She then proceeded to New York City, arriving in March 1816 and playing no further part in the events of the Pacific fur trade.

Wilson Price Hunt set off from Saint Louis at the head of the overland expedition on October 21, 1810. At just 27, he was an unlikely choice to lead an overland expedition on this scale. With no expertise in wilderness travel, the criteria for his appointment was solely his proven business acumen and his American citizenship. Assisting him was Donald Mackenzie, a former employee of the North West Company. The Hunt party departed St. Louis in October 1810, a month after the *Tonquin* sailed out of New York harbor.

The objective of the overland expedition was, in essence, to conduct a reconnaissance in order to locate suitable sites for a string of trading posts extending from the Missouri River to the Columbia. The expedition comprised a small group of company officials and partners, and about 50 employees. In the end, however, the ineptly led and poorly planned expedition fared no better than those who approached the Columbia mouth by sea.

Hampered by needless mistakes and blunders, solely the consequence of inexperience, hostile natives, and scheming rivals, the Hunt party meandered and dithered, unnecessarily enduring hunger and thirst, freezing cold, and death as they struggled across barren expanses crossing the continental divide. Across the continent, they encountered both friendly and hostile tribes, created inter-cultural difficulties through their own inexperience, and fell prey to harsh conditions by failing to respect the seasonal calendar that dictated transcontinental travel. Hunt's group departed in the early winter for Fort Osage, 450 miles up the Missouri River from their starting base, Nodawa Camp, 15 miles from St. Joseph. To their misfortune, the company timed the most important seasonal calculations on the basis of avoiding the expense of supporting employees through an idle part of the year. From Osage, they wandered west with an erratic sense of long-term expectations, in a "haphazard fashion."[26] The group consisted of 59 persons

— 58 men and one woman; four were company partners. The first segment of the overland journey was on schedule, and all appeared well.

Departing from Nodawa, they headed up the Missouri River early enough in the spring to reach winter camp short of the Rocky Mountains at the right time of year. By late spring, Hunt reached the Omaha Village, where he received news that a band of Yankton and Lakota Sioux were blocking their path ahead. At their meeting, tensions rose, and the opposing parties took up positions on opposite banks of the Missouri. Hunt carried two company howitzers and one swivel gun, firing them in an attempt to intimidate the Sioux, who signaled for parlay with buffalo robes. In the peace talks that ensued, the Sioux explained that they were at war with the Arikara, Mandan, and Gros Ventres (Big Belly). After much effort, Hunt convinced them that his party was traveling to the western ocean and had no interest in Sioux lands. This was found to be acceptable, and the expedition continued.

Among Hunt's most egregious mistakes was his continuation of running afoul of seasonal weather. Having departed from St. Louis in the early winter, there was a chance of crossing the highest western ranges during the following spring. However, a few hundred miles out, he returned to St. Louis to settle pending transactions and to recruit Pierre Dorion, the only member who could speak Siouxan languages. On the return to reunite with the party at Osage, he wasted days while Dorion fought with his wife, at times beating her mercilessly and causing her to disappear for extended periods. With her came two boys, and she spent part of the journey pregnant with a third. In addition, Dorion was heavily in debt to Manuel Lisa of the Missouri Fur Company, and Lisa was loath to let it go. Along Hunt's route, Lisa pursued the expedition, beginning 19 days and 240 miles behind. Once Hunt and Dorion were confronted with the debt, the ensuing tensions almost resulted in a duel. Some modest agreement was reached, but the companies generally avoided mutual interactions, including attacks on Arikara villages and the natural reprisals. These considerations plagued the party all the way west.

The first to reach the log palisades of Fort Astoria staggered in sometime in January 1812, with the remainder arriving in one and twos over the course of the following weeks and months. Two missing members, John Day and Ramsay Crooks, were later found along the Columbia River, stripped naked by Indians and left stranded without even flints to make a fire. The experience apparently drove John Day insane, and he died a year later. While the disastrous expedition certainly found no practical route between the Missouri and Columbia Rivers, it did serve to reinforce the modest American presence in the Pacific Northwest.

Now known as the Astorians, members of the Pacific Fur Company spread out from the mouth of the Columbia River to explore and commence the exploitation of the fur trading resources of the wide hinterland. Fort Okanogan was founded, making it the first structure and settlement to fly the American flag in the future state of Washington, and Fort Spokane was located within sight of the North West Company's Spokane House. In mid-1812, a seven-man party led by

Robert Stuart returned by the overland route from Fort Astoria to New York. By directing their route slightly south of that followed by Hunt and his expedition, Stuart discovered what came to be known as South Pass in central Wyoming, which proved to be a practical route across the Rocky Mountains and later a key component of the Oregon Trail. For fear of competition, however, the details of this route were not immediately made public.

Stuart

The Chinook were not always willing to work as guides or messengers to other tribes situated at great distances. Through this reluctance, they often delayed the Astorians from making important introductions before the North West Company intruded and undermined them. On one occasion, the tribe escorted Francois Benjamin Pillet up the Columbia a short way, but abruptly refused to go any farther after small exchanges with the Skilloots near the mouth of the Cowlitz River. He made the dubious declaration that seasonal flooding would prohibit further travel, and Pillet was forced to return to the settlement. Nevertheless, Astoria placed great importance on retaining the Lower Chinook as the resident middlemen. Concomly provided Astoria with fish once the ceremonial catches were complete. Salmon was a basic source of nutrition, and the Hawaiian talent for fishing was put to good use as a "constant task"[27] while the salmon were in season. The Europeans, however, grew discontented with a fish-based diet. Roosevelt elk and black-tailed deer were seen from time to time, but not in large enough numbers for a reliance on a steady supply of meat. Concomly introduced the settlement to wapato root, an important staple

---

[27] *Revolvy*

for the winter. An excellent substitute for potatoes, they were brought in such quantity that storage cellars had to be built. The Chinook displayed a talent for weaving, and trappers purchased tightly interwoven hats to keep out the cold. Not only was the weaving waterproof, but wide enough to cover the shoulders. As a peripheral attraction, expertly woven animal images were included in the texture. Whether these images carried a spiritual significance or expressed an artistic bent is unknown.

Despite the Pacific Fur Company's success with Concomly and the Lower Chinooks, Britain's North West Company solidified its hold on the market through the establishment of numerous inland posts, such as the Spokane House, Kootenai House, and Saleesh House. These were located far up the Columbia where it turns directly toward the north, hundreds of miles from Astoria. However, it was a region to be exploited, and the Americans immediately affirmed their intention to build there as well. Almost immediately, they responded with a flanking maneuver by soliciting a trade connection with Russian America more rapidly than expected. The effort resulted in a "beneficial agreement"[28] by which Russia would greatly augment American trading supplies. The agreement was intended to prevent Montreal's presence in the region. Russia's distaste for such a close British presence was a boon for Astor's company's dealings with the far north. From colonial times, the eastern part of the continent was dominated by the Hudson's Bay Company and several French enterprises. Such was Hudson Bay's scope that were it to stake a claim in the West, it could dominate the entire coast alongside the North West Company. At that point, the British claim to land would take on a stark reality for an American president intent on connecting the two oceans.

Scarcely a month after the *Tonquin*'s arrival, the commercial functions of Fort Astoria were already producing results and establishing a presence in the Columbia Basin as the prospective "Emporium of the West."[29] However, the actual supply and residence structures, situated only a few miles from the Lewis and Clark winter quarters at Fort Clatsop, were barely begun. Terrain and thick forests made clearing the land a Herculean task. The standing timber of the coastal Columbia is thick and tall, with heavy underbrush. Few among the party had ever swung an axe, and none had logging experience. The trees were swathed in hardened resin, slowing progress even further, and removing stumps seemed all but impossible. Typically, four men stood on a platform at least eight feet above the ground to cut each tree, and the slow pace continued at a rate of one tree per two days. The settlement had no resident medical officer, and almost as a rule, one half of the available personnel was unable to work due to a variety of illnesses.

Still, despite the ubiquitous presence of the North West Company, Astor's Pacific Fur Company held the most strategically practical and defendable location in the Pacific Northwest, and such discomforts would not drive them out. The earliest American settlement in the West

---

[28] *Revolvy*

[29] *Revolvy*

between Spain's San Francisco and Russian America, Astoria's initial success fit in well with Astor's intent to complement international sea trade via a string of forts across the American continent, using American tribes as suppliers.

As intended, small parties fanned out from Astoria in the following months to establish trade relations with various inland tribes. The first interior routes always began by traveling directly eastward upriver. Within a month or two following Tonquin's arrival, Captain Thorn grew restless to fulfill the ship's part of the bargain and departed for the north coast as per Astor's instructions. On June 5, the day of her departure, only a small part of the settlement had been successfully completed, but Thorn could wait no longer. His itinerary included a voyage all the way to Russian America to meet with Alexander Baranov at New Arkhangel (modern-day Sitka). There, he was to trade supplies and a large number of gunpowder barrels before returning to the Columbia and on to foreign markets.

Of the new posts built throughout the region, one of the nearest to Astoria was the Wallace House of what is now Keizer, Oregon, in the Salem area of the Willamette Valley. Also known under the name of Fort Calapooya after the local tribe, Wallace House became an important source for beaver pelt and much-needed venison to feed the Columbia settlement. Unlike Astoria, the Willamette Valley was abundant in elk and white-tailed deer. Wallace House was founded by a party of 14, led by William Wallace and John Haisley, and the group wintered over in the valley, returning to Astoria almost two years later with nearly 800 beaver pelts. What the residents of Wallace House did not expect was an entire new spate of allergies and diseases that thrive in the Oregon country's high humidity. The Willamette Valley was dubbed by tribes who had lived there for centuries as the "valley of a thousand fevers," and European descendants often had difficulty coping with the natural conditions. Astoria itself fared scarcely better, with the cold, humidity, and alien features of the environment.

Of the distant posts, among the most prominent was the fort established at the confluence of the Columbia and the Okannakken (in modern usage, Okanogan). To reach the junction, the first party took 42 grueling days, but the established facility became the first such post built by Americans in the future state of Washington. This was Astor's response to the North West Company's Spokane House and other northeastern posts. The North West Company enjoyed a two-year advantage over him in the area, building its impressive facility close to modern-day Spokane. Rival companies often built their posts in proximity to one another without heightened tensions. All understood that the same resources were sought, regardless of the post's location. Companies often preferred to have the competition situated nearby for social interaction through the long seasons. However, in the case of Fort Okanogan, opposite North West's Spokane House, a council was held with the leaders of the Okanogan tribe, and an official agreement was forged in order to maintain friendly relations. Under ordinary circumstances, this might not have been necessary. However, far to the east, tensions were rising between Britain and the U.S. that would result in a coming war. The council was well worth the trouble, as the American group produced a harvest of 2,500 beaver pelts by the following spring.

Fort Okanogan

Jon Roanhaus' picture of the site of the fort

Relations between traders and regional tribes varied greatly. Perhaps the most welcoming and pacifistic relationship was held with the Syilx at the mouth of the Okannakken. Astorians, in fact, received an official invitation from the eastern northwest tribe to live with them as members of the community. The message was delivered by Kauxama Nupika, described by her tribe as a "two-spirit." Kauxama was a woman of extremely tall, muscular stature who claimed that the supernatural powers of the white man had changed her into a male. She took a wife and engaged in male roles and rituals, including horse stealing and fighting. It is ironic that her message to the Astorians was an invitation for a peaceful life, despite her reputation for sudden, unexpected violence.

Even for the Chinook guides and interpreters, communication with the Syilx and their Nysilxcom language was problematic. The Okanogan Trail followed by the Astorians was known to the Syilx as Nkwala's Trail in honor of their chief. The tribal invitation invited the trappers to live in the large native encampment or to build a trading post, with the accompanying exhortation to "always be our friends."[30]

---

[30] *Revolvy*

The process of reaching the Okanogan was met with less goodwill from a few of the other tribes. Portaging at night, the Astorians found themselves in a morning skirmish with the Wascos. John Reed was injured while protecting the party's supplies, and a large box holding company dispatches for Astor was stolen. A clerk brought on board by Hunt, Reed was entrusted with the personal delivery of settlement documents to the company founder. The attack occurred along the way. Two attackers were reportedly killed in the struggle, and the Chinook returned later in large numbers. Stuart was able to negotiate a settlement of six blankets and tobacco before continuing up the river. Reed was able to reach Fort Okanogan for medical attention by April 24.

By the third week of July, David Stuart led a party of eight men into Syilx Territory. In a collaboration based on self-preservation, Astorian and North West members traveled together to The Dalles, presently 80 miles from the city of Portland. Contact was made with several tribes along the way, and although the Chinook were the most helpful for arranging meetings, their good will was erratic. Around The Dalles, the Astorians met with the Watlala Chinook, and try as they might, could not manage to establish good relations. For their trouble, the Chinook "performed several military displays"[31] in an effort to intimidate the Europeans and stole a fair amount of goods from their supply. Fortunately, the trappers were offered protection from the Watlala by the Wasco-Wishram chiefs. Farther upriver, the party found success in trading salmon for horses with the Chelan. Despite the difficulty of the Okanogan route, the full establishment of the Pacific Fur Company's post there was complete by the following year. Astor's project still lagged two years behind the North West Company. British posts had been erected in British Columbia, Montana, and Idaho. However, this did not seem to trouble Astor unnecessarily, as he had already made a large fortune in trade with the Chinese and still believed that he would come to control the Pacific Northwest. Routes would soon open between Russian America to the Quing Empire in China. Astor's ships were poised to sail for Gangzhou.

Not all inland trade routes emanating from Astoria involved following the Columbia. To the north were as many unfamiliar tribes as there were to the east. On May 12, 1811, David Stuart led a party with the assistance of Calpo, a Clatsop guide, northward after a brief trek east up the Columbia. In the settlement's first departure from the Columbia, Stuart explored the Cowlitz River and at one bend encountered a massive flotilla of Cowlitz warriors. MacKay was able to successfully achieve parlay and learned that the gathering had armed itself for combat against the nearby Skilloot village, near the river's mouth. The Stuart party was, for the time being, safe. Meanwhile, in the same week, the group moving eastward up the river arrived in what is now The Dalles. There, they discovered the most important fishery of the entire river, what was later known as Celilo Falls, eventually lost to the Dalles Dam. The Dalles struck the expedition as one of the most ideal spots on the river for a trading fort, and they were shocked that no one had ever

---

[31] *Revolvy*

attempted it. Despite the opportunity, they were forced to retreat back to Astoria, as Calpo would not continue. He feared reprisals against him and his people from the Wishram-Wasco tribe.

In early June, Stuart led another party north along the coast of present-day Washington, again with Calpo leading the way. The party reached the Olympic Peninsula with its high mountain range, where Stuart spoke with several tribal leaders. Most were subsets of the large coastal Salishan nation extending from the Columbia to Vancouver Island and inland to Puget Sound. The languages, however, differed in each region. Stuart's party returned to Astoria within three weeks with good news from the Quinault and Quileute. These two tribes offered to kill sea otters and trade pelts for valuable Dentalium shells commonly sold by the Nuuchalnulth on Vancouver Island. Stuart was desirous of a new trading post at what is now Gray's Harbor on the northern coast. He had good reason to believe that the Alutiiq, as far north as Russian America, could be recruited to hunt various fur-bearing animals as well. These could easily be sent to the southern factory of Astoria for preparation and shipping.

Ironically, all of the overland parties' efforts to cross the continent put them in Astoria at a time in which the settlement was threatened with extinction by rekindled hostilities between the U.S. and Britain. Some claim that the War of 1812 was merely the next chapter of the Revolutionary War, but in actuality, new issues were at stake. The bulk of the action took place along the eastern seaboard into the northern country near Niagara to the Great Lakes regions. At sea, the impressive British Royal Navy continued to take American sailors by force off their ships and press them into British service. The American government fought the "impressment"[32] of American military personnel, despite being hopelessly overmatched in terms of naval strength. In the north, the two countries fought over the constantly changing Canadian border. To secure Canadian land, the protection of some American states would benefit from a buffer. For the British, Canada was the beginning of an enormous new empire, rife with resources in the Western Hemisphere.

For the U.S., to declare war upon Britain, despite being a leonine task, was timely, as most of the English naval resources were taken up with the fight against Napoleon. On the American continent, the British were creating an unstable system of alliance with the numerous inland and coastal tribes. This created a dilemma for West Coast concerns, as the trade of iron tools, blankets, and beads for pelts was the chief resource of the country west of the Louisiana Purchase.

Despite its stark unpreparedness for another war and the national distaste for funding a standing army, it was the only time in which British naval resources could be distracted by other conflicts. The crown was in possession of over 600 warships, while the U.S. had 16 vessels properly outfitted for conflict at sea. In terms of British fur companies operating in the West, two

---

[32] Louise Arthur Norton, *The Pacific in the War of 1812: Pelts, Ploys and Plunder* – www.file:///C:/Users/George/Download:10677-38391-1-PB.pdf

were given permission to claim global fur rights in many parts of the world, including the Pacific coast. That the North West Company lacked a royal charter was of no consequence in the moment.

With the slow travel of news in the early 19th century, life went on as it had in the West, oblivious to faraway events. The Astorians knew nothing of these occurrences. Even disconcerting rumors took months to reach the West, and Astoria was living a peaceful existence through the remainder of 1812. However, the North West Company was informed of the state of war far earlier than the Americans. They were also informed of Britain's decision to send a warship to the Columbia's mouth to destroy the settlement. On October 13, 1813, George McTavish and a party of 73 men in 10 canoes landed in Astoria. Representing the North West Company, they brought a warning that the HMS *Racoon* was on its way to effect the settlement's capture.

For McTavish, the visit was a stern diplomatic mission, but a commercial treasure trove as well. The traders were aware that fighting a British force was impossible due to the loss of the *Tonquin* and the unknown whereabouts of the *Beaver*. With low numbers and few weapons, the settlement was a "garrison in name only."[33] The Astorians' only recourse, in lieu of warfare, was to sell the entire stockpile of their beaver pelts to McTavish and the North West Company for a small fraction of the market value. Following the transaction, some members left the area, either awaiting a ship to the Pacific or setting out across the continent on a return trip to St. Louis and points north.

Once Astor caught wind of British intentions toward his settlement, he corresponded with President Monroe at once, requesting that a force of at least 40-50 men be sent immediately to the coast for protection. In his plea, he reminded Monroe that America would be sorry to lose its precious "infant establishment"[34] in the long run. With more pressing matters on his schedule, Monroe entirely ignored Astor. However, the businessman wrote the president again when he discovered that Britain was sending one or more ships to be directed by the North West Company. Madison agreed to Astor's request and set aside one well-equipped ship to rescue the Western investment.

Monroe's gesture was not trivial. The *Adams* was a 28-gun frigate of the U.S. Navy with a stellar history against Barbary pirates and French privateers in the West Indies, recapturing stolen vessels. In 1812, she was restructured to an additional length of 15 feet and equipped with heavier guns.

Monroe intended to alter her intended voyage to the Great Lakes for the sake of Astoria, but before departure, her mission to the West was postponed. Her crew was transferred to Lake

---

[33] *Louise Arthur Norton*

[34] *Louise Arthur Norton*

Ontario for other U.S. and British conflicts. Astor, forever on watch for an advantage, had begun to outfit a second ship to serve as a supply vessel for *Adams* and to do the same for Astoria upon her arrival. He was devastated at the breakdown of Monroe's plan.

The Pacific Fur Company was, by 1813, "functionally defunct,"[35] and the Astorians had little else to do but continue trade for as long as they could. Having already reached the Nez Perce in the Walla Walla Valley, despite the tribe's reluctance to meet Pacific Fur Company prices, John Clarke went a step further. Traveling from the Spokane River into the Palouse Valley to the northeast of Walla Walla, he entered the realm ruled by Chief Palus, a legendary and beloved figure in the region. The prospects for successful trading began well. Clarke brought with him two silver goblets solely for the purpose of impressing the Indians. In ceremonial fashion, he poured wine in both and drank together with the Chief. Just as a good outcome seemed imminent, the goblets were stolen by a tribal member. Rather than save the good will produced by the meeting, Clarke recovered the goblets and saw to it that the thief was hung. The resulting anger toward all white men plagued trade in the region for decades. The tribes of the Palouse had "long memories"[36] and revisited the matter long after the Pacific Fur Company was gone, complicating the trade aspirations of the North West Company.

The North West Company, uncertain as to the HMS *Racoon's* position, sent a second ship under their charge, the Isaac Todd, to capture Astoria. The Isaac Todd carried the necessary papers to legally seize the settlement, and several accompanying ships sailed in support. However, on April 11, 1813, McTavish returned to Astoria, first to inform the traders there that the British ship was still coming and that it might be near. No more able to fight than they had been months before, the Astorians offered no resistance and treated the 'Nor'westers' as honored guests. They freely provided food for the British trappers, and the companies agreed to suspend all manner of competition. The Astorians were given a fair time in which to make an orderly evacuation. The Racoon finally arrived with a captain who was outraged over having no one to fight and nothing to capture, since the settlement of Astoria was once again occupied with British personnel. On June 13, the remainder of supplies and the whole of the facility was sold to the North West Company, and the settlement was renamed Fort George by its new British owners.

With the arrival of the HMS *Racoon*, the remainder of Astoria property was liquidated. On November 12, 1813, the American flag was hauled down, and the Union Jack raised, signifying the reestablishment of Fort George. In an opportunistic moment, the captain of the *Racoon* took the liberty of claiming the entire Oregon Country as a protectorate of the British Empire. The Isaac Todd arrived in April of the following year, with little to do except in support of the new British management as it benefited the North West Company. Despite its intent to destroy the settlement, the Isaac Todd agreed to take along two Pacific Fur Company agents at its departure.

---

[35] *Revolvy*

[36] *Native American Networks*

In an unhappy reminder of the dangers faced at their arrival, both Alexander Henry and Donald McTavish drowned when their boat capsized on their way to the ship.

A painting of Fort George

In certain instances, the British were less successful in establishing tribal relations, coming under attack by various groups. A number of Pacific Fur Company personnel remained in the Northwest, although a few original members of Astor's overland party attempted a return to St. Louis using the newly discovered South Pass. John Reed relocated, building a home at the confluence of the Boise and Snake rivers. He was killed in 1814 on that property by Bannocks, along with visitor Pierre Dorion. Marie Dorion and her children were spared and eventually reached Fort Okanogan by the following spring.

As for Astor, his wealth continued to grow as the war drew to a close, in part through a lucrative bond deal forged with the U.S. government. The loss of Astoria caused no small amount of frustration to its namesake, but it was not overly significant in financial terms. His New York City investments skyrocketed, and the parent American Fur Company was eventually sold.

In some small comfort to Americans on the Pacific, the Treaty of 1818 returned American property to its original owners. The claim of ownership regarding the Oregon country was partially retracted, establishing a policy of "joint occupancy"[37] in which both sides agreed to not

---

[37] *Infogalactic, Pacific Fur Company – www.infogalactic.com/info/Pacific_Fur_Company*

inhibit the other. The disputed boundaries dissolved three decades later, and Britain vacated the Pacific Northwest.

Several individual accounts from the original members were unearthed in the decades following Astoria's demise. Each offers some detail on narrow slices of life within the Pacific Fur Company. William Wallace Matthews sailed on the *Tonquin*, but he was not present at her destruction. He stayed in Astoria after the disintegration of the settlement, spent almost two years on the Okanogan, and in his writings, detailed the search for a better British position on Tongue Point. He married Kilakotah, daughter of Chief Cohaway, and had a daughter named Ellen. Despite this, he took an active part in capturing and hanging two Indians accused of murder.

The annals left by Duncan McDougall, who supervised the post for two years, include daily entries on routine life and economic prosperity within the settlement. These are the most synchronous accounts with actual events. MacDougall offers a somewhat altered account of the Tonquin's demise and claims that the ship's interpreter was Jack Ramsay. Most believe that it was George Ramsay. The permanent residents of Astoria, following its collapse, are listed, but three died too soon to be considered established settlers. Those who remained include William Canning, Alexander Carson, John Cox, Lieutenant Baptiste Dorion, Marie L'Auguivoise Dorion, Jean-Baptiste Dubrieul, Joseph Gervais, Sailor Jack, Louise L. Bonte, Michel La Framboise, Etienne Lucier, Jean Baptiste Desporte MacKay, Thomas MacKay, Francoise Fayette, and George Ramsay. Judge Archibald Pelton, the New Englander found by the Shahaptian Indians, was at last brought back into the settlement's fold. He managed to find later employment with the North West Company, but he never fully regained his sanity, and a band of the Clatskanie tribe murdered him three years after his arrival. The Russian ship's carpenter, Johann Koster, left the Columbia River in 1815. However, while the ship was still in sight of the Columbia bar, he "became suddenly insane"[38] and jumped overboard. Virginian John Day, for whom a major river in central Oregon is named, began a return to St. Louis overland, but upon becoming temporarily insane, he was taken back to Astoria and remained there.

Donald MacKenzie's grandson, Carl, wrote extensively on his grandfather's account of Astoria's last days. Much of his research was dedicated to proving that the elder MacKenzie was not responsible for the sale of the Pacific Fur Company's assets to the Northwest Company. He supported his contention by affirming that MacKenzie "retained the friendship of John Jacob Astor,"[39] and that he was "the best trader in the Pacific Northwest."[40] Employing only one source, the volume is described by one historian as "tiresome reading."[41]

---

[38] *J. Nielsen Barry, Astorians Who Became Permanent Settlers, The Washington Historical Quarterly, Vol. 34, No. 3 (July, 1933, University of Washington, p. 223*

[39] *Cecil W. MacKenzie, King of the Northwest, the Story of an International Hero of the Oregon Country and the Red River Settlements at Lower Fort Garry (Winnipeg), Review by J. Turnbull, Oregon Historical Quarterly, Vol. 39 No. 1, (March 1938) p.79*

[40] *Cecil W. MacKenzie*

[41] *Cecil W. MacKenzie*

Astoria owed a debt of gratitude to sailor Joseph Ashton, who was more experienced in navigation of the Northwest than any other man at the settlement. He alone understood that a white flag flown from the foremast signified a North West Company ship, not a sign of surrender. In the final days of Astoria, he warned the traders that the same signal would likely be employed by the HMS *Racoon* or any other British warship. Ashton was put in charge of "rigging the Dolly,"[42] a vessel once used by the Pacific Fur Company. While attending to repairs, he was fond of shooting ducks from the deck, causing him to be attacked by Indians. From that point on, he was assigned four Hawaiian guards. Called "Old Joe" by his colleagues and carrying a reputation for extraordinary truthfulness, the middle-aged Ashton was the oldest of the working members of the settlement.

Surprisingly, little biographical information has been forthcoming about the personal and business workings of Astor's personality until the interim between World War I and World War II in the 20th century. By the end of his involvement in the fur trade in 1834, even the Southwest Fur Company ceased its operations in the Upper Midwestern region. Astor had become the first American millionaire on record. At his death in 1848, his total wealth was estimated at a figure approaching $20 million, the equivalent of $800 million today. His prominence as a business tycoon was matched by his role in fulfilling Jefferson's long-range dreams of a continental nation. His awareness of investment's relationship with national and global politics was keen, evidenced by the fact that during the War of 1812, he mounted relief efforts under both the American and British flags. Through this, he remained immune to resistance from either country.

Astor left the great bulk of his fortune to his son, plus a sum of $400,000 with which to found a library in his name, and that institution ultimately became the New York City Public Library.

In terms of modern equivalents, Astor died as the fifth wealthiest man in American history.

Online Resources

Other books about colonial history by Charles River Editors

Further Reading

"Acquisitions: Fur Trade: The North West Company." Hudson's Bay Company Heritage. (Accessed December 19, 2016.)

Allen, Laura. "The Price of a Feather." *National Parks Conservation Association*, 2015. https://www.npca.org/articles/918-the-price-of-a-feather. Accessed 7 July 2020.

"American Fur Company." *Wikipedia*, 2020. en.wikipedia.org/wiki/American_Fur_Company/. Accessed 17 July 2020.

---

[42] *Kenneth W. Porter, Joseph Ashton, Astorian Sailor, Oregon Historical Quarterly, Vol. 31 No. 4 (December 1930) pp. 343,344*

Andra-Warner, Elle. *Hudson's Bay Company Adventures: Tales of Canada's Fur Traders*. Heritage House Publishing Co., 2011.

Backhouse, Frances. *Once They Were Hats. In Search of the Mighty Beaver*. Toronto: ECW Press, 2015.

Bakker, Peter. *A Language of Our Own: The Genesis of Michif, the Mixed Cree-French Language of the Canadian Métis*. New York: Oxford University Press, 1997.

Benz, Stephen. "Savior of the Snowy Egrets." *Interdisciplinary Studies in Literature and the Environment* 7 (2) Summer 2000, pp. 224-234.

Blum, Dilys. "Ahead of Fashion: Hats of the 20th Century." *Philadelphia Museum of Art Bulletin* 89, Summer 1993. 1-48.

Brown, Jennifer. "Beaver Pelts," *The Canadian Encyclopedia*.

Bryce, George. "The Old Settlers of Red River." Lecture to a Meeting of the Manitoba Historical Society: MHS Transactions, Series 1, No. 19, November 26, 1885.

Carlos, Ann M. and Lewis, Frank D. *Commerce by a Frozen Sea: Native Americans and the European Fur Trade*. Philadelphia: University of Pennsylvania Press, 2010.

Campbell, Henry Colin. "Radisson and Groseilliers: Problems in Early Western History". *The American Historical Review,* 1896.

"Charter and supplemental charter of the Hudson's Bay Company." Hudson's Bay Company. Project Gutenberg. (Accessed 26 November 2016).

Coutts, Robert and Stuart, Richard, ed. "The Forks and the Battle of Seven Oaks in Manitoba History." *Manitoba Historical Society*, 1994.

"Deed of Surrender." Hudson's Bay Company Heritage. (Accessed December 20, 2016).

"Dr. John Rae" Hudson's Bay Company Heritage. Accessed December 19, 2016.

"Dome Petroleum Limited." *Historica Canada.* 1985- (Accessed December 20, 2016.)

Douglas, Thomas. *Observations on the Present State of the Highlands of Scotland: With a View of the Causes and Probable Consequences of Emigration*. (London: Longman, Hurst, Rees, and Orme, 1805), 171-172.

"Early Stores." Hudson's Bay Company Heritage. (Accessed December 20, 2016.)

Galbraith, John S. *Hudson's Bay Company, 1821-1869, Volume 1*. Berkeley: University of California Press, 1957.

"Gold Rush Fever in B.C. 1858-63". Canada, A Country by Consent. West/Dunn Productions. <http://www.canadahistoryproject.ca/1871/1871-05-gold-rush.html>

Henderson, Anne Matheson. "The Lord Selkirk Settlement at Red River, Part 1." *Manitoba Pageant*, Autumn 1967, Volume 13, Number 1.

Hogue, Michel. *Metis and the Medicine Line: Creating a Border and Dividing a People*. Chapel Hill, NC: University of North Carolina Press, 2015.

Houston, Stuart C. and Houston, Mary I. "Manitoba History: The Sacking of Peter Fidler's Brandon House, 1816," *Manitoba History*, Number 16, Autumn 1988.

Hunt, George T. *The Wars of the Iroquois: A Study in Intertribal Trade Relations*. Madison, WI: University of Wisconsin Press, 1940.

"Hudson's Bay Company Announces Seven New Locations in The Netherlands." Hudson's Bay Company Press Release. Toronto and Amsterdam, 11 July 2016.

Laut, Agnes Christina. *Pathfinders of The West: Being the Thrilling Story of The Adventures of The Men Who Discovered the Great Northwest*: Radisson, La Vérendrye, Lewis and Clark. New York: The Macmillan Company, 1904.

The Lord Selkirk Association of Rupert's Land. Newton, Stan *Mackinac Island and Sault Ste. Marie*. Mackinaw: Sault News Printing Company, 1909.

Martin, Joe. "Conflict at Red River: Collision at Seven Oaks." *Manitoba Historical Society*, 1994.

Maton, William F. *Canadian Constitutional Documents: A Legal History*. 1994.

Morton, W.L "The North West Company: Pedlars Extraordinary." *Minnesota History*, Winter 1966.

"The North West Company." Hudson's Bay Company Heritage. Accessed December 19, 2016.

Nute, Grace Lee. "Chouart Des Groseilliers, Médard," in *Dictionary of Canadian Biography*, vol. 1, University of Toronto/Université Laval, 2003-. Accessed November 24, 2016.

Ogg, David. *England in the Reign of Charles II, Vol. 1*. Oxford: Clarendon Press, 1934.

"Our History." Hudson's Bay Company Heritage. (Accessed December 20, 2016.)

"People: Explorers: Radisson and des Groseilliers." Official Website of the Hudson's Bay Company. (Accessed 23 November, 2016.)

"Prince Rupert". *Encyclopaedia Britannica*, s.v. Chicago: 2007.

Rankin, Laird "Nonsuch Gallery." The Manitoba Museum. www.manitibamuseum.ca (Accessed 26 Nov. 2016).

"Red River Colony", Education Scotland: Scots and Canada. Accessed December 17, 2016.

"Richard Burbidge." Hudson's Bay Company Heritage. (Accessed December 20, 2016.)

Royot, Daniel. *Divided Loyalties in a Doomed Empire: The French in the West: From New France to the Lewis and Clark Expedition.* Newark, DE: University of Delaware Press, 2007.

"Rupert's Land Act, 186 - Enactment No.1." *Canada's System of Justice.* Government of Canada, Department of Justice.

"Sir George Simpson." Hudson's Bay Company Heritage. Accessed December 19, 2016.

Smith, Shirlee Anne. "Rupert's Land" In *The Canadian Encyclopedia. Historica Canada,* 1985–. (Accessed 12 Dec., 2016.)

"The Story of the Nonsuch." The Manitoba Museum. www.manitibamuseum.ca (Accessed 26 Nov. 2016).

Waldram, James Burgess, Herring, Ann T., and Kue Young. *Aboriginal Health in Canada: Historical, Cultural, and Epidemiological Perspectives.* Toronto: University of Toronto Press, 2006.

Warkentin, Germaine Pierre-Esprit. *Radisson: The Collected Writings, Volume 1: The Voyages.* Toronto: The Champlain Society, 2012.

W.B. Coltman Report Transcription. Library and Archives Canada. September 30, 2016.

26545503R00038